Thanks to

my esteemed Gurus

Naam Eagam Kaaja Bawa

&

Lama Zopa Rinpoche

Wishes from

His Eminence Lama Zopa Rinpoche

May this book become sunshining of dispels the darkness of the sky, the ignorance of sentient being from where all the suffering confusion comes,

With much Love and prayer

Zopa

24/1/2023

Art of Inner Luminous

THE HOLY THOUGHTS OF SPIRITUAL INCENSE

The Eternal Monk AJAYHRITIK

ISBN
Paperback 979-8-89363-340-5
Hardcase 979-8-89415-336-0

'Age is just a number!'

The author is a perfect example of this quote. The 18-year-old is spiritually mature to make people understand the concepts of inner thoughts.

At the tender age of 18, Ajayhritik emerged as a beacon of spiritual insight, defying expectations and demonstrating a profound understanding of the mystical tapestry of existence. Born into a world pulsating with the energy of the digital age, he embarked on a journey of self-discovery that would lead to the weaving of spiritual wisdom into the fabric of his young life.

From the earliest recollections of childhood, Ajayhritik exhibited an innate curiosity about the unseen dimensions of life. Surrounded by technology and a cacophony of modern distractions, he sought solace in introspection, contemplating the cosmos and the essence of the human spirit. The search for meaning became his compass, guiding him through the labyrinth of youthful challenges.

Harnessing the power of the digital era, he seamlessly integrated spirituality into the virtual landscape.

Through social media platforms and an insightful blog, he shared reflections on mindfulness, meditation, and the interconnectedness of all things.

The written word became his chosen medium for expressing the ineffable. Even in the bustling tumult of high school life, he found moments to transcribe profound insights, creating a repository of personal reflections that would later blossom into his first literary endeavours.

In a world often preoccupied with superficial ideals, he embraced authenticity as his guiding principle. Vulnerable and unfiltered, he openly shared his own struggles, transforming his writing into a mirror that reflected the shared human experience. The result was a body of work that resonated with readers across the globe, creating connections forged in the crucible of sincerity.

As the author stands at the cusp of adulthood, the world eagerly anticipates the unfolding chapters of his life and literary career. The story of the 18-year-old spiritual author is not just a biography but a testament to the limitless potential of the human spirit, capable of transcending age and illuminating the path toward profound understanding and enlightenment.

Table of Contents

NOTE

“This spiritual book is a profound journey into the realms of personal introspection and spiritual exploration, as it unfolds exclusively through the lens of the author's own experiences. By grounding the teachings in personal anecdotes, the book offers readers an intimate glimpse into the author's soul-searching quest and the transformative power of spirituality in their life. This approach fosters a sense of authenticity, encouraging readers to embark on their spiritual journey with the understanding that wisdom can be found not only in ancient scriptures but also in the lived experiences of individuals. Through this deeply personal lens, the book becomes a guiding light, inviting readers to reflect on their own spiritual path and embrace the universal elements that connect us on our quest for meaning and enlightenment.”

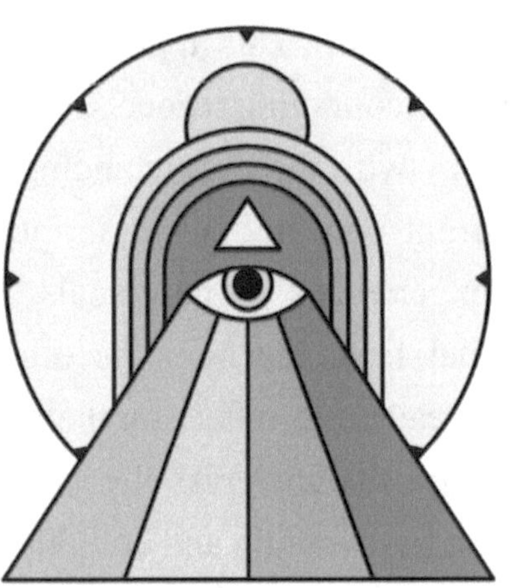

Introduction: The Call to Spirituality

In the profound silence of our innermost being, where the echoes of our yearnings reverberate, lies the subtle yet undeniable call to spirituality. It is beckoning us to embark on a transformative journey beyond the tangible realms of our existence, seeking a connection that transcends the boundaries of the material world. This book, nestled in the cradle of introspection and guided by the whisperings of the soul, responds to that call with an unwavering commitment to explore the depths of the spiritual terrain. Through the chapters that follow, we will navigate the intricate pathways of personal discovery, drawing wisdom from the wellspring of individual experiences. As we heed the call to spirituality, this narrative becomes a compass, offering insights, reflections, and timeless teachings that illuminate the way. Join us on this sacred expedition, where the journey is as important as the destination and where the soul's longing finds solace in the embrace of spiritual exploration.

Setting the Stage for the Spiritual Journey

Introduction to the Spiritual Landscape

Embarking on a spiritual journey is akin to stepping into uncharted territory within ourselves. Before delving into the intricacies of this transformative expedition, it is essential to set the stage for the spiritual journey—a sacred space where seekers can cultivate awareness, understanding, and a deeper connection to the essence of their existence.

The Quest for Meaning

At the heart of setting the stage for a spiritual journey is the recognition of the human quest for meaning. Spirituality provides a framework to explore the profound questions that echo through the corridors of our consciousness, inviting us to discover purpose and significance beyond the surface of our daily lives.

Defying Simple Definitions

Defining spirituality proves to be a nuanced endeavour. It defies simplistic categorisations, for it is an intimate and multifaceted experience that varies from person to person. This complex nature is an inherent aspect that sets the tone for a journey that demands openness and receptivity to diverse perspectives.

Beyond Religious Boundaries

Spirituality transcends the confines of religious dogma. While religious traditions may offer pathways to spiritual insights, the setting we establish acknowledges that the spiritual journey is not confined to any particular set of beliefs. It is a universal expedition, inviting individuals from various faiths and backgrounds to explore the common threads woven into the fabric of spiritual understanding.

Connection to the Transcendent

At its core, spirituality involves seeking a connection to the transcendent—a realm beyond the tangible and material. Whether one conceptualises this as a divine force, cosmic energy, or the interconnectedness of all things, this dimension sets the stage for a journey into the mysteries that lie beyond our immediate senses.

A Personal and Subjective Exploration

Defining spirituality must encompass its deeply personal and subjective nature. It is a journey within oneself, an exploration of the inner landscape where personal truths unfold. This recognition lays the groundwork for an odyssey that values individual experiences, insights, and revelations as integral components of the broader spiritual tapestry.

The Universality of Human Experience

The setting for our spiritual journey acknowledges the universality of human experience. By recognising that, regardless of cultural or geographical differences, the fundamental questions about existence, purpose, and the nature of reality are shared, we create a space that transcends superficial distinctions and fosters unity.

Liberation from Dogma

Our stage is free from the confines of rigid dogmas. Liberating spirituality from strict ideological structures allows for a more fluid and inclusive exploration. The spiritual journey is not limited by predefined doctrines but rather opens itself to the richness of diverse traditions and perspectives.

Harmonising Science and Spirituality

An essential aspect of the stage we set is the harmonious interplay between science and spirituality. Instead of viewing these realms as conflicting, we embrace the idea that they can coexist and complement each other. This acknowledgement encourages seekers to explore the intersections where empirical knowledge and metaphysical understanding converge.

The Metaphysical Landscape

Delving into the metaphysical aspects of spirituality enriches the setting for our journey. It involves exploring concepts beyond the tangible, such as consciousness, interconnectedness, and the subtle energies that permeate the universe. This dimension invites seekers to venture into the depths of the unknown with open minds and receptive hearts.

A Holistic Perspective

In establishing the stage, we encourage a holistic perspective that considers the mind, body, and spirit as interconnected facets of the human experience. This holistic approach recognises that the spiritual journey involves not only intellectual exploration but also a deep integration of mind, body, and soul.

Transcending Dualities

Spirituality, as we define it, encourages the transcendence of dualities. It invites seekers to move beyond the polarities of right and wrong, good and bad, and embrace a more nuanced understanding of the complexities inherent in the human experience. This departure from binary thinking creates a foundation for a more compassionate and inclusive journey.

Inner and Outer Exploration

The setting for the spiritual journey encourages a balance between inner and outer exploration. While the journey unfolds within the depths of one's consciousness, it is also an exploration of the external world. This dual focus recognises that spiritual insights are not confined to solitary introspection but can also be found in the tapestry of everyday experiences.

Embracing Mystery and Uncertainty

Setting the stage involves acknowledging and embracing the mystery and uncertainty inherent in the spiritual journey. It is an expedition into the unknown, where answers may be elusive, and the path may unfold in unpredictable ways. This acceptance of ambiguity fosters resilience and adaptability, vital qualities for the spiritual seeker.

Connection to Nature and the Cosmos

Spirituality often involves a profound connection to nature and the cosmos. The stage we set encompasses the recognition that the natural world, with its rhythms, cycles, and beauty, serves as a source of inspiration and spiritual insight. This connection expands the scope of the journey beyond individual consciousness to the vastness of the universe.

Cultivating Mindfulness

An essential element of the spiritual journey's stage is the cultivation of mindfulness. This involves being fully present in the moment, attuning oneself to the subtleties of experience, and fostering a deep awareness of one's thoughts, emotions, and surroundings. Mindfulness becomes a guiding light, directing the seeker's attention to the richness of the present.

Sacred Practices and Rituals

- In crafting the setting, we recognise the significance of sacred practices and rituals. Whether drawn from established religious traditions or personal rituals, these practices serve as anchors that ground the spiritual journey. They offer a tangible means for seekers to express devotion, gratitude, and reverence along the way.

The Role of Community

The spiritual journey is not a solitary endeavour but often involves a sense of community. The stage we set acknowledges the importance of connecting with like-minded individuals, mentors, or spiritual guides. This communal aspect provides support, shared insights, and the understanding that the journey is enriched through collective wisdom.

Symbolism and Archetypes

In setting the stage for the spiritual journey, we delve into the realms of symbolism and archetypes. Recognising the power of symbols and archetypal imagery, we understand that they can serve as potent tools for transcending language and accessing deeper layers of the psyche. These symbolic elements enrich the narrative of the journey with layers of meaning and resonance.

Opening the Heart

The spiritual journey is as much about opening the heart as it is about expanding the mind. Our setting encourages seekers to cultivate qualities of compassion, empathy, and love. This heart-centred approach fosters a deeper connection not only with oneself but also with others, creating a more inclusive and harmonious spiritual landscape.

Surrender and Letting Go

Central to the stage we set is the recognition of the power of surrender and letting go. The spiritual journey often involves releasing attachments, relinquishing control, and trusting in the unfolding of the path. This surrender is not an act of weakness but a profound acknowledgement of the vast intelligence that guides the journey.

Integration of Shadow and Light

The spiritual journey is a process of integrating both the shadow and the light aspects of the self. Our setting embraces the understanding that true spiritual growth involves confronting and embracing the darker aspects of one's psyche. By integrating the shadow, seekers move toward a more holistic and authentic expression of their being.

Cultivating Gratitude

An essential element of the spiritual journey is the cultivation of gratitude. Our stage encourages seekers to appreciate the richness of life, acknowledging both the challenges and the blessings along the way. Gratitude becomes a transformative force, shaping the perspective of the journey and fostering a sense of abundance.

Reflection and Contemplation

Setting the stage involves creating spaces for reflection and contemplation. Whether through meditation, journaling, or silent moments of introspection, the seeker is invited to pause and navigate the depths of their inner landscape. These moments of stillness allow for a deeper understanding of the self and the unfolding journey.

The Endless Quest

As we conclude the exploration of setting the stage for the spiritual journey, we acknowledge that the quest is endless. The stage is not a static backdrop but a dynamic landscape that evolves with each step of the journey. The seeker, now equipped with a foundation that encompasses diverse perspectives and dimensions, steps into the vast and boundless terrain of spiritual exploration, ready to discover, learn, and grow.

Defining spirituality

Spirituality is a multifaceted and deeply personal concept that defies a singular definition, as it encompasses a wide range of beliefs, practices, and experiences. At its core, spirituality involves a search for meaning, purpose, and connection to something beyond the material realm. It transcends religious affiliations and institutional boundaries, allowing individuals to explore their inner selves and the larger, often ineffable, aspects of existence.

One key element of spirituality is the quest for a higher power or ultimate reality. This can take various forms, such as a divine being, cosmic energy, or a universal consciousness. Individuals often turn to spirituality as a means of finding guidance, solace, and a sense of belonging in a world that can be complex and challenging.

Spirituality is not confined to organised religions, and many people identify as spiritual without adhering to specific dogmas or doctrines. It is a subjective and experiential journey that emphasises personal growth, self-discovery, and the cultivation of virtues like compassion, love, and mindfulness. Spirituality encourages individuals to look inward, reflecting on their thoughts, emotions, and actions, and fostering a sense of inner peace and harmony.

The practice of mindfulness and meditation is often intertwined with spirituality. These techniques allow individuals to quiet the mind, become more aware of the present-moment, and develop a deeper understanding of themselves. Through these practices, people may experience a heightened sense of connection with the world around them and a greater appreciation for life.

Spirituality also involves a moral and ethical dimension, guiding individuals to live in accordance with values that transcend the materialistic and ego-driven aspects of life. Many spiritual traditions emphasise the importance of kindness, generosity, and compassion towards others, promoting a sense of interconnectedness and collective well-being.

The concept of transcendence is central to spirituality, suggesting a movement beyond the ordinary and a connection to something greater than oneself. This can manifest as a transcendent experience during meditation, prayer, or moments of awe in nature, leading to a profound sense of unity and interconnectedness with the cosmos.

In the realm of spirituality, rituals and ceremonies play a significant role. These may vary widely among different cultures and belief systems but often serve as symbolic expressions of the spiritual journey. Rituals can provide a sense of structure, community, and continuity in the pursuit of the sacred.

Spirituality is not limited to an individual's personal life but can extend to the collective and societal levels.

Communities may form around shared spiritual values, fostering a sense of belonging and support. Moreover, spiritual perspectives can influence social justice movements, environmental activism, and other efforts to create a more compassionate and equitable world.

The exploration of existential questions, such as the meaning of life, suffering, and death, is a fundamental aspect of spirituality. Different spiritual traditions offer diverse answers to these questions, providing individuals with frameworks to navigate the complexities of human existence and find purpose in their lives. The relationship between spirituality and religion is intricate. While spirituality can exist independently of organised religions, many religious traditions incorporate spiritual elements. However, spirituality allows for a more personal and flexible approach, accommodating diverse perspectives and interpretations of the sacred.

Spirituality is a dynamic and evolving concept, adapting to the changing needs and beliefs of individuals over time. As people encounter new experiences, engage in self-reflection, and interact with diverse cultures, their spiritual perspectives may shift and deepen, contributing to ongoing personal growth. Despite its personal nature, spirituality can foster a sense of interconnectedness and shared humanity. It encourages individuals to recognise the divine or sacred not only within themselves but also in others, promoting empathy, tolerance, and a sense of unity that transcends cultural, religious, and societal differences.

Ultimately, defining spirituality is a deeply personal and subjective endeavour. It encompasses a rich tapestry of beliefs, practices, and experiences that defy easy categorisation. Spirituality invites individuals to embark on an inward journey, exploring the mysteries of existence, seeking meaning, and cultivating a connection to something beyond the tangible and mundane aspects of life.

Significance of Spirituality in Modern Life

Spirituality holds immense significance in the complexity of modern life, providing a compass for individuals navigating the challenges and uncertainties of the contemporary world. In a society characterised by rapid technological advancements, globalisation, and a constant influx of information, spirituality offers a grounding force that resonates on various levels.

Inner Harmony

Spirituality serves as a pathway to inner harmony, offering a refuge from the hustle and bustle of modern living. Amidst the noise, it encourages individuals to find moments of stillness and self-reflection.

Coping with Stress

The demands of modern life often lead to stress and anxiety. Spiritual practices, such as meditation and mindfulness, become invaluable tools for managing and mitigating these mental health challenges.

Meaning in a Material World

In a materialistic culture, spirituality provides a framework for seeking meaning beyond material possessions. It prompts individuals to question the deeper purpose of their existence.

Interconnectedness in Isolation

Despite technological connectivity, many individuals experience a sense of isolation. Spirituality fosters a profound sense of interconnectedness, emphasising the understanding that all life is intertwined.

Ethical Navigation

The moral compass provided by spirituality becomes crucial in an era where ethical dilemmas are pervasive.

It guides individuals in making choices aligned with their values and principles.

Community Building

Spiritual communities offer a haven for like-minded individuals seeking shared values and a sense of belonging. In an era of virtual connections, these communities provide tangible support networks.

Compassion in a Divisive World

Spiralling political and social divisions characterise the modern world. Spirituality promotes compassion, urging individuals to empathise with diverse perspectives and fostering a more inclusive society.

Mind-Body Integration

Amidst the emphasis on technological progress, spirituality underscores the importance of the mind-body connection.

Resilience in Adversity

Life's challenges are inevitable, and spirituality becomes a wellspring of resilience. It equips individuals with the tools to navigate adversity and bounce back from setbacks.

Adapting to Change

The rapid pace of change in the modern world can be disorienting. Spirituality encourages adaptability and acceptance, allowing individuals to flow with the currents of change.

Gratitude in Consumer Culture

Consumer culture often fuels desires for more. Spirituality counters this by promoting gratitude and encouraging individuals to appreciate the present-moment and the blessings they have.

Self-Discovery Amidst Noise

In a world inundated with information and external stimuli, spirituality offers a path to self-discovery. It prompts individuals to tune into their inner selves amidst the cacophony of external influences.

Balancing Act

Modern life often skews the work-life balance. Spirituality advocates for equilibrium, emphasising the importance of nurturing personal, professional, and spiritual dimensions of life.

Environmental Stewardship

Many spiritual traditions underscore the sacredness of the environment. In an age of ecological challenges, spirituality becomes a driving force for sustainable practices and environmental stewardship.

Inspiration for Creativity

Spirituality has historically been a wellspring of inspiration for artists, writers, and creators. It taps into a realm beyond the mundane, fuelling creative expression.

Holistic Education Paradigm

Integrating spiritual principles into education can create a more holistic learning environment, addressing not only academic development but also the emotional and spiritual growth of individuals.

Conflict Resolution Through Compassion

In a world marred by conflicts, spiritual principles advocate for non-violent and compassionate conflict resolution, fostering peace and understanding.

Cultural Harmony

Spirituality contributes to cultural harmony by promoting acceptance and appreciation of diverse cultural traditions, fostering a world where different beliefs coexist harmoniously.

Mindful Tech Usage

As technology infiltrates every aspect of life, spirituality encourages mindful technology use. It calls for a balanced approach that leverages the benefits of technology without losing sight of human connection.

Social Justice Catalyst

Many social justice movements find inspiration in spiritual principles. Spirituality becomes a catalyst for change, motivating individuals to advocate for justice, equality, and human rights.

Health and Healing Connection

The link between spirituality and improved health outcomes is increasingly recognised. Practices like prayer and meditation contribute to physical, mental, and emotional well-being.

Support in Addiction Recovery

Spirituality often plays a pivotal role in addiction recovery programmes, providing a source of strength and support for individuals seeking to overcome substance abuse.

Addressing Existential Questions

In an era where existential questions loom large, spirituality provides frameworks for grappling with the mysteries of existence, mortality, and the purpose of life.

Preserving Cultural Identity

Spiritual traditions contribute to the preservation of cultural heritage, offering a sense of continuity and identity amidst the rapid global homogenisation of cultures.

Humanising Technology Through Ethics

Spirituality contributes to humanising technology by emphasising the importance of ethical considerations in its development and use. It urges a tech landscape aligned with human values, compassion, and empathy.

Awakening the Soul: Understanding Spiritual Awakening

Introduction to Spiritual Awakening

Spiritual awakening is a profound and transformative experience that transcends the ordinary aspects of life. It is often described as a journey towards self-discovery, heightened consciousness, and a deep connection with the divine. Awakening the soul involves a shift in perception, a realisation of a greater truth beyond the material world.

The Nature of the Soul

The soul, in spiritual terms, is considered the eternal and unchanging essence of an individual. Awakening the soul implies becoming aware of this inner self, understanding its purpose, and aligning one's life with its wisdom. It goes beyond religious boundaries, emphasising a universal connection between all living beings.

The Catalysts of Awakening

Spiritual awakening can be triggered by various life events such as profound moments of clarity, intense emotional experiences, or a search for meaning and purpose. These catalysts serve as wake-up calls, prompting individuals to question their existence and embark on a journey of inner exploration.

The Role of Mindfulness and Presence

Mindfulness and being present in the moment are crucial aspects of spiritual awakening. By cultivating awareness of thoughts, emotions, and sensations, individuals can break free from the confines of the ego and connect with a deeper, more authentic self.

Inner Transformation

Awakening the soul is not just about acquiring knowledge but about a profound inner transformation. This transformation may lead to a shift in values, priorities, and perspectives, influencing how individuals relate to themselves, others, and the world around them.

The Dark Night of the Soul

Many spiritual traditions acknowledge a challenging phase known as the 'Dark night of the soul,' where individuals confront their deepest fears, doubts, and insecurities. This period of inner turmoil is considered a necessary step toward true spiritual awakening, leading to greater self-awareness and resilience.

Spiritual Practices and Disciplines

Various spiritual practices and disciplines, such as meditation, prayer, yoga, and mindfulness, serve as tools for awakening the soul. These practices create a conducive environment for self-discovery, enabling individuals to tap into the limitless potential of their spiritual essence.

Integration of Spirituality into Daily Life

True spiritual awakening extends beyond moments of insight or enlightenment; it involves the integration of spiritual principles into everyday life. This integration is reflected in one's actions, relationships, and the way challenges are approached.

Service and Compassion

A fully awakened soul often leads to a sense of purpose rooted in service to others. Compassion becomes a guiding force, and individuals find fulfilment in contributing positively to the well-being of others and the world, recognising the interconnectedness of all life.

In conclusion, awakening the soul is a profound and multifaceted journey that encompasses self-discovery, ego dissolution, inner transformation, and a deep connection with the universal essence. It is a process that transcends religious boundaries, inviting individuals to explore the depths of their inner selves and embrace a higher consciousness that can profoundly shape their lives and the world around them.

Exploring the Concept of Spiritual Awakening

Spiritual awakening is a transformative process that transcends conventional understanding and opens individuals to a heightened sense of self-awareness, interconnectedness, and spiritual consciousness. It is a concept deeply rooted in various religious and philosophical traditions, emphasising a profound shift in perception and an awakening to a higher reality.

The Universality of Spiritual Awakening

Despite the diversity of religious beliefs and cultural backgrounds, the concept of spiritual awakening is universal. It is an innate human experience that can manifest in various forms, driven by an intrinsic human longing for meaning, purpose, and connection with something greater than the self.

Awakening as a Personal Journey

Spiritual awakening is a highly personal journey, and its manifestations can differ widely among individuals. While some may undergo sudden and dramatic transformations, others may experience a gradual unfolding of awareness over an extended period.

The Nature of Reality

One key aspect of spiritual awakening is a shift in perception regarding the nature of reality. Individuals often question the limitations of the material world and seek a deeper understanding of the spiritual dimensions that underlie existence.

Mind-Body-Spirit Connection

Spiritual awakening involves recognising and harmonising the interconnectedness of the mind, body, and spirit. This holistic approach acknowledges that spiritual growth encompasses not only intellectual understanding but also emotional, physical, and intuitive aspects of being.

Breaking Free from Egoic Patterns

Ego dissolution is a central theme in many spiritual traditions. Awakening involves transcending egoic patterns of thought and behaviour, allowing individuals to perceive themselves and the world with greater clarity, compassion, and humility.

The Role of Consciousness

Consciousness plays a pivotal role in spiritual awakening. The expansion of consciousness involves an awareness that extends beyond individual identity, fostering a sense of unity with all living beings and the cosmos.

Interplay of Faith and Doubt

The journey of spiritual awakening is characterised by a delicate interplay between faith and doubt. Individuals grapple with uncertainties, question established beliefs, and navigate a path that requires trust in the unknown.

Awakening and Religion

Spiritual awakening is not exclusive to any particular religion. While religious frameworks may provide a foundation, awakening often transcends dogma, encouraging a direct, personal experience of the divine or transcendent reality.

Mystical Experiences and Transcendence

Mystical experiences are frequently reported during spiritual awakenings, involving a direct encounter with the divine, a sense of unity with the cosmos, or an overwhelming feeling of transcendence beyond the constraints of time and space.

The Importance of Presence and Mindfulness

Central to the process of spiritual awakening is the practice of presence and mindfulness. Being fully present in the moment allows individuals to break free from the distractions of the past and future, fostering a deeper connection with the present reality.

Awakening and Empathy

Spiritual awakening often enhances empathic abilities. As individuals become more attuned to their inner selves, they develop a heightened sensitivity to the emotions and experiences of others, fostering greater compassion and empathy.

Synchronicity and Signs

Many individuals report experiencing synchronicities or meaningful signs during their spiritual awakening. These events, often perceived as guidance from a higher intelligence, serve as affirmations on the path of self-discovery.

Cultural and Global Implications

As more individuals undergo spiritual awakening, there are potential cultural and global implications. A collective shift in consciousness may influence societal values, fostering a greater emphasis on cooperation, environmental stewardship, and compassion.

Awakening and Creativity

Spiritual awakening is closely linked to heightened creativity. As individuals connect with their inner source of inspiration, they often experience a surge in creative expression, whether through art, music, literature, or other forms of self-expression.

The Illusion of Separation

Spiritual awakening challenges the illusion of separation, emphasising the interconnectedness of all life. This recognition has profound implications for how individuals relate to others, the environment, and the world at large.

Transcending Dualities

Spiritual awakening involves transcending dualistic thinking—moving beyond concepts of good and bad, right and wrong. This shift in perspective allows individuals to embrace a more holistic understanding of existence.

Role of Teachers and Guides

Spiritual teachers and guides often play a significant role in the awakening process. Their wisdom, guidance, and support can provide clarity, reassurance, and a sense of direction during the sometimes-tumultuous stages of awakening.

Ecstasy and the Blissful States

Some individuals experience states of ecstasy and bliss during spiritual awakening. These heightened states of consciousness are often described as moments of union with the divine, providing a profound sense of joy and fulfilment.

Awakening and Timelessness

Spiritual awakening often brings a sense of timelessness. The emphasis shifts from the past and future to an appreciation of the eternal present, fostering a profound acceptance of the unfolding of life in its natural rhythm.

The Ongoing Journey

Spiritual awakening is not a destination but an ongoing journey. As individuals continue to explore the depths of their inner selves, they contribute to the collective evolution of human consciousness, fostering a more enlightened and interconnected world.

Discussing the Signs of Organic Awakening

'Organic Awakening' generally refers to a natural and spontaneous process of spiritual or personal awakening that occurs without the influence of external factors such as religious doctrines, specific practices, or intentional seeking. It is a term often used to describe a more intuitive and innate form of awakening that arises from within. Here, we'll discuss some signs associated with what is commonly referred to as 'Organic Awakening.'

Intense Self-Reflection

Individuals experiencing an organic awakening often find themselves engaged in profound self-reflection. They start questioning the meaning and purpose of their lives, pondering existential questions, and seeking deeper understanding of their own identity.

Heightened Awareness

There is an increased sensitivity to the world around them. This may include a heightened awareness of nature, a deeper connection with other people, and a more profound understanding of the interconnectedness of all things.

Shift in Values

A noticeable shift in personal values often accompanies an organic awakening. Materialistic pursuits may lose significance, and individuals may prioritise qualities like compassion, love, and authenticity in their lives.

Synchronicities

People undergoing an organic awakening frequently report experiencing synchronicities—meaningful coincidences that seem to align with their inner journey. These synchronicities are often interpreted as signs that they are on the right path.

Spontaneous Moments of Clarity

Unlike structured spiritual practices, those experiencing an organic awakening may have spontaneous moments of clarity or profound insight. These insights often come without warning and may lead to a deeper understanding of life and existence.

Connection with Intuition

There's an increased reliance on and trust in intuition. People going through an organic awakening may find themselves making decisions based on inner guidance rather than relying solely on external information or societal expectations.

Changes in Relationships

Relationships may undergo transformation during an organic awakening. There may be a desire to surround oneself with like-minded individuals who share a similar spiritual or philosophical outlook. Alternatively, existing relationships may evolve as individuals become more authentic in their interactions.

Inner Peace Amidst Chaos

Despite external challenges, those experiencing an organic awakening often report a newfound inner peace. This inner calmness becomes a stabilising force, allowing individuals to navigate life's ups and downs with greater resilience.

Creativity and Expression

An organic awakening often unleashes creative energy. Individuals may feel a heightened desire to express themselves through art, music, writing, or other creative endeavours as a means of exploring and sharing their newfound insights.

Acceptance and Letting Go

There's a growing acceptance of life as it is, accompanied by a willingness to let go of attachments and expectations. This sense of surrender allows individuals to flow more gracefully with the natural unfolding of their journeys.

Alignment with Natural Rhythms

Those undergoing organic awakening may find themselves more attuned to the natural rhythms of life. This could involve a greater appreciation for nature, an awareness of seasonal changes, and a recognition of the cyclical nature of existence.

Non-Attachment to Labels

Individuals in the midst of an organic awakening often become less attached to labels, whether they be societal roles, religious affiliations, or other identity markers. There is a recognition that these labels do not define the essence of who they truly are.

Gratitude and Appreciation

A deep sense of gratitude often accompanies an organic awakening. Individuals may develop an appreciation for the simple joys of life and find gratitude in the midst of both challenges and blessings.

It's important to note that these signs are not necessarily sequential, and the experience of organic awakening can vary greatly from person to person. Each individual's journey is unique, and the signs mentioned here are general indicators that someone may be undergoing a natural and spontaneous process of awakening.

Experiences Associated With Awakening

Experiences associated with awakening are diverse and can vary widely among individuals. Spiritual or personal awakening involves a profound shift in consciousness, leading to a deeper understanding of oneself, the interconnectedness of all things, and a higher or more expansive reality. Here are some key experiences often associated with the awakening process:

Expanded Consciousness

A fundamental aspect of awakening is an expansion of consciousness. Individuals may experience a heightened awareness that transcends the ordinary perception of reality. This expanded consciousness often leads to a deeper understanding of the interconnectedness of all life.

Moments of Profound Clarity

Awakening is marked by moments of profound clarity and insight. These moments can be spontaneous and may provide individuals with a deeper understanding of their purpose, the nature of existence, and the path they are meant to follow.

Synchronicities

Many people undergoing awakening report experiencing synchronicities—meaningful coincidences that seem to align with their inner journey. These events are often perceived as signs or affirmations that individuals are on the right path.

Heightened Intuition

Awakening often brings about a heightened sense of intuition. Individuals become more attuned to their inner guidance, relying on intuition to make decisions and navigate their lives.

Loss of Egoic Identification

A significant aspect of awakening involves a shift away from egoic identification. Individuals may experience a dissolution of the ego, leading to a less rigid attachment to self-image, personal achievements, and external validation.

Profound Inner Peace

Despite external challenges, individuals undergoing awakening often report profound inner peace. This peace arises from a deep acceptance of the present-moment and a surrender to the natural flow of life.

Connection with a Higher Self or Divine Presence

Awakening may involve a sense of connection with a higher self, universal consciousness, or a divine presence. This connection often leads to a feeling of guidance and support on the spiritual journey.

Loss of Fear of Death

As individuals awaken to a broader understanding of existence, they often experience a diminished fear of death. The recognition of life as a continuous, interconnected process contributes to a more peaceful perspective on mortality.

Emotional Release and Healing

Awakening can trigger emotional release and healing. Individuals may revisit past traumas, unresolved emotions, or limiting beliefs, allowing for a process of healing and emotional liberation.

Timelessness and Present-Moment Awareness

A shift in perception regarding time is common during awakening. Individuals may experience a sense of timelessness and a heightened awareness of the present-moment, emphasising the importance of living in the now.

Transcendent and Mystical Experiences

Some individuals undergoing awakening report transcendent or mystical experiences. These may include a sense of oneness with the universe, encounters with divine beings, or moments of ecstasy and bliss.

Intense Inner Turmoil (Dark Night of the Soul)

The awakening process is not always blissful; it may involve a phase of intense inner turmoil known as the 'Dark night of the soul.' During this challenging period, individuals confront deep-seated fears, doubts, and uncertainties.

Heightened Sensitivity and Empathy

Awakening often leads to heightened sensitivity and empathy. Individuals become more attuned to the emotions and experiences of others, fostering a deeper sense of compassion and connection.

Non-Attachment to Outcomes

Awakening frequently results in a decreased attachment to specific outcomes and a greater acceptance of the natural ebb and flow of life. This non-attachment allows for a more flexible and resilient approach to challenges.

Integration of Dualities

Individuals undergoing awakening often experience a shift in their perception of dualities—moving beyond concepts of good and bad, right and wrong. This integration allows for a more holistic understanding of existence.

It's crucial to recognise that the awakening journey is highly individualised, and not everyone will have the same experiences. Additionally, these experiences may not occur in a linear fashion, and individuals may revisit or deepen certain aspects of their awakening over time.

The Inner Path: Navigating the Spiritual Journey

The Inner Path represents a profound journey of self-discovery and spiritual exploration, transcending the external world to delve into the depths of one's inner being. Navigating this spiritual journey involves a commitment to self-awareness, introspection, and a willingness to confront both the light and shadow aspects of the self. The Inner Path is not a prescribed route but a personal exploration where individuals seek to understand the essence of their existence, the nature of consciousness, and their connection to the greater cosmos.

Embarking on the Inner Path requires a departure from external distractions and a turning inward, often facilitated by practices such as meditation, mindfulness, and introspective contemplation. It is a journey that unfolds beyond the confines of religious dogma, emphasising a direct and personal connection with the sacred or transcendent.

The Inner Path is marked by the integration of spiritual principles into daily life, fostering a harmonious balance between the material and spiritual realms. It involves aligning one's actions with inner wisdom, compassion, and a deep sense of purpose. As individuals traverse this path, they often encounter challenges, confront limiting beliefs, and undergo transformative experiences that contribute to their spiritual growth.

On the Inner Path, the concept of time takes on a different dimension, emphasising the importance of living in the present-moment. It involves a continuous process of letting go of attachments, surrendering to the flow of life, and embracing the evolving nature of the self. The Inner Path is not a destination but a perpetual journey of evolution and self-realisation.

Guidance from spiritual teachers, wisdom traditions, and personal insights gleaned from the inner journey serve as invaluable companions on the Inner Path. These sources provide a roadmap, but each individual must ultimately forge their unique route based on personal revelations and a deep connection with the inner self.

In essence, navigating the Inner Path is an ongoing, dynamic process of self-exploration and spiritual evolution. It invites individuals to uncover the profound truths that lie within, leading to a transformative journey where the self becomes a reflection of the sacred and the spiritual becomes an integral part of everyday life.

Mapping Out Each Stage in the Path

While the spiritual path is highly individualised and may not follow a linear progression, it often involves certain stages of growth and self-discovery. Here's a brief mapping of each stage in the spiritual path:

Awakening

The journey often begins with an awakening—a moment of realisation or insight that prompts a deep questioning of life's purpose and one's own existence. This phase involves a heightened awareness and a desire for deeper understanding.

Seeking

Following awakening, individuals often enter a seeking phase, exploring various spiritual traditions, practices, or teachings. This stage involves a thirst for knowledge, attending workshops, reading spiritual texts, and engaging in practices like meditation or yoga.

Learning and Exploration

During this stage, individuals actively engage in learning about different spiritual concepts and philosophies. They explore a variety of practices, seeking those that resonate most with their inner truth. This phase often involves introspection and self-study.

Inner Healing

As individuals progress, they may encounter a phase of inner healing. This involves confronting and addressing past traumas, limiting beliefs, and emotional wounds. Inner healing is essential for personal growth and the development of a more authentic self.

Ego Dissolution

The spiritual path often includes a critical stage of ego dissolution, where individuals begin to transcend the egoic mind. This involves letting go of the attachment to self-identity, pride, and the need for external validation. It paves the way for a more profound connection with the inner self and the collective consciousness.

Transcendence

In this stage, individuals may experience moments of transcendence—moving beyond ordinary states of consciousness. This can manifest as a sense of unity with the divine, a deep connection to all of creation, or profound mystical experiences.

Integration

Following moments of transcendence, the integration stage involves bringing these insights and realisations into everyday life. It's about embodying spiritual principles, living authentically, and aligning one's actions with inner wisdom. This stage emphasises the fusion of the spiritual and material aspects of life.

Non-Duality

Advancing further, some may enter a phase of non-duality. This stage involves a deep understanding that all dualities—such as good and bad, self and other—are ultimately illusions. It fosters a sense of oneness and unity with all of existence.

Mastery and Continued Growth

The spiritual journey is ongoing, and mastery involves a continuous commitment to growth, learning, and deepening one's spiritual connection. Individuals may become guides or mentors, sharing their wisdom and experiences with others on the path.

It's important to note that individuals may move through these stages at different paces, revisit certain stages, or experience them in a different order. The spiritual path is a dynamic and individualised journey, and these stages provide a general framework rather than a rigid roadmap.

Challenges Faced During the Voyage

The spiritual voyage is a profound and transformative journey, but it is not without its challenges. Here are some common challenges individuals may face during their spiritual journey:

Resistance to Change

Embracing a spiritual path often requires significant changes in mindset, habits, and lifestyle. The resistance to change, both from within and from external influences, can create challenges as individuals navigate unfamiliar territories.

Egoic Resistance

The ego, with its attachment to identity and self-image, may resist the dissolution that comes with spiritual growth. Facing and overcoming egoic resistance can be a significant challenge on the path to self-realisation.

Dark Night of the Soul

Many spiritual traditions recognise a phase known as the 'Dark night of the soul.' This is a period of intense inner turmoil, doubt, and existential crisis. Navigating through this challenging phase requires resilience, faith, and self-compassion.

Loneliness and Isolation

The spiritual journey can be a solitary quest, and individuals may experience feelings of loneliness or isolation, especially if their evolving beliefs and perspectives differ from those around them.

Doubt and Uncertainty

Doubt about the validity of the spiritual path or uncertainty about the future may arise. Trusting the process and staying committed despite doubts can be a significant challenge.

Confronting Shadow Self

The journey often involves facing and integrating the shadow self—the darker, hidden aspects of one's personality. Confronting and transforming these aspects can be emotionally and psychologically challenging.

Attachment to Spiritual Experiences

Individuals may become attached to particular spiritual experiences or states of consciousness. The challenge lies in not clinging to these moments but understanding that the spiritual path is dynamic and experiences may vary.

Overcoming Addictions and Habits

Spiritual growth may necessitate overcoming unhealthy habits or addictions that hinder progress. Breaking free from these patterns can be a difficult but necessary part of the journey.

Balancing Spiritual and Material Realms

Integrating spiritual insights into everyday life can be challenging. Balancing the demands of the material world with spiritual principles requires conscious effort and mindfulness.

Loss of Familiar Identity

As individuals progress on the spiritual path, they may experience a loss of the familiar identity constructed by societal norms, roles, and expectations. Adjusting to this shift can be disorienting.

Facing Unresolved Trauma

The spiritual journey often involves revisiting and resolving unresolved traumas. This process can be emotionally intense and may require the support of mental health professionals or spiritual guides.

Cultural and Social Challenges

Some individuals may face resistance or judgement from cultural or religious communities that do not align with their evolving spiritual beliefs. This can create a sense of conflict and isolation.

Maintaining Consistency in Practice

Establishing and maintaining consistent spiritual practices, such as meditation or mindfulness, can be challenging amidst the demands of daily life. Discipline and commitment are essential.

Spiritual Bypassing

Spiritual bypassing occurs when individuals use spiritual concepts to avoid facing unresolved emotional issues. Recognising and addressing these issues authentically is crucial for genuine spiritual growth.

Comparison and Spiritual Pride

Comparing one's spiritual progress to others or developing spiritual pride can hinder the humility and openness necessary for continued growth. Cultivating a sense of equality and shared humanity is essential.

Navigating these challenges requires resilience, self-reflection, and a willingness to confront discomfort. Seeking guidance from experienced mentors, connecting with like-minded communities, and integrating spiritual insights into practical life are essential strategies for overcoming the obstacles on the spiritual voyage.

Offering Guidance for Those Beginning Their Journey

Embarking on a spiritual journey is a transformative and rewarding experience. Here are some guidance and suggestions for those who are beginning their spiritual journey:

Start with Self-Reflection

Begin by reflecting on your life, values, and beliefs. Ask yourself deep and meaningful questions about the purpose of your existence and what brings you true fulfilment.

Set Intentions

Clarify your intentions for the spiritual journey. Define what you hope to gain, whether it's inner peace, self-discovery, or a connection to a higher purpose. Having clear intentions will guide your path.

Explore Different Paths

There are various spiritual traditions, practices, and philosophies. Explore different paths to find what resonates with you. Attend workshops, read books, and engage with different communities to broaden your understanding.

Cultivate Mindfulness

Incorporate mindfulness into your daily life. Practice being fully present in the moment, whether through meditation, deep breathing, or simply paying attention to your surroundings. Mindfulness is a foundational aspect of the spiritual journey.

Be Open-Minded

Approach your spiritual journey with an open mind. Be willing to challenge preconceived notions, beliefs, and societal conditioning. Open-mindedness allows for a more expansive and authentic exploration.

Connect with Nature

Spend time in nature. Nature has a profound way of connecting us to the present-moment and grounding us in a deeper sense of awareness. Take walks, hike, or simply sit in stillness, surrounded by the beauty of the natural world.

Seek Guidance

Consider seeking guidance from spiritual teachers, mentors, or communities. Experienced individuals can provide insights, share their wisdom, and offer support as you navigate the challenges and discoveries on your journey.

Practice Gratitude

Cultivate a sense of gratitude for the present-moment and the experiences that come your way. Gratitude fosters a positive mindset and helps you appreciate the beauty in both simple and profound aspects of life.

Journaling

Keep a spiritual journal to document your thoughts, insights, and experiences. Writing can be a powerful tool for self-reflection and tracking your growth throughout the journey.

Practice Self-Compassion

Be kind and patient with yourself. The spiritual journey may involve facing challenging aspects of your inner self. Embrace the process with self-compassion, understanding that growth takes time and is part of the human experience.

Integrate Spiritual Practices

Incorporate spiritual practices into your routine. This could include meditation, prayer, yoga, or any other practice that resonates with you. Consistency in these practices can deepen your connection to the spiritual aspects of life.

Be Aware of Egoic Patterns

Pay attention to egoic patterns and tendencies. The ego may resist change and cling to familiar ways of thinking and behaving. Awareness of these patterns allows you to navigate them with greater understanding.

Embrace Challenges as Opportunities

Challenges are inherent in any spiritual journey. View them as opportunities for growth and learning. Embracing challenges with an open heart can lead to profound insights and transformation.

Join Spiritual Communities

Connect with like-minded individuals by joining spiritual communities, either in person or online. Sharing experiences and insights with others can provide valuable support and a sense of belonging.

Celebrate Small Wins

Acknowledge and celebrate the small victories and moments of growth along the way. Recognising progress, no matter how incremental, reinforces your commitment to the spiritual journey.

Remember, the spiritual journey is a personal and evolving process. Be patient, stay curious, and embrace the unfolding path with an open heart and mind. Each step you take is a valuable part of your unique and transformative journey.

Meditation and Mindfulness: Tools for Spiritual Growth

Meditation and mindfulness are powerful tools for spiritual growth, offering a pathway to deeper self-awareness, inner peace, and a profound connection with the essence of life. Here's an exploration of how meditation and mindfulness serve as essential tools on the spiritual journey:

Cultivating Presence

Meditation and mindfulness emphasise being fully present in the current moment. By focusing attention on the breath, bodily sensations, or the immediate environment, individuals learn to cultivate a heightened state of presence, breaking free from the distractions of the past or anxieties about the future.

Inner Stillness and Silence

Through regular meditation practice, individuals learn to quiet the mind and experience moments of inner stillness and silence. This inner calmness provides a space for reflection, self-discovery, and a direct connection with the deeper aspects of the self.

Observing Thoughts and Emotions

Both meditation and mindfulness encourage the non-judgemental observation of thoughts and emotions. This practice helps individuals develop a more detached and objective perspective on their inner experiences, fostering a greater understanding of the patterns of the mind.

Stress Reduction

Mindfulness meditation has been widely recognised for its stress-reducing benefits. By bringing attention to the present-moment, individuals can create a mental space that allows for a healthier response to stressors, promoting emotional resilience and well-being.

Deepening Self-Awareness

Meditation and mindfulness are tools for deepening self-awareness. Through introspection, individuals can explore their motivations, desires, fears, and beliefs, gaining insights into the core aspects of their identity and contributing to personal and spiritual growth.

Connection with the Breath

Focusing on the breath is a common meditation technique that promotes a sense of grounding and connection with the present. The breath becomes a metaphor for the ebb and flow of life, reminding individuals of their connection to the universal rhythm.

Mind-Body Connection

Mindfulness practices often involve paying attention to bodily sensations and the breath. This awareness fosters a stronger mind-body connection, helping individuals become attuned to the physical manifestations of their emotions and thoughts.

Developing Compassion

Compassion meditation, a subset of mindfulness practices, involves cultivating feelings of empathy and kindness towards oneself and others. This nurtures a compassionate attitude that extends beyond personal boundaries, fostering a sense of interconnectedness and spiritual growth.

Enhancing Focus and Concentration

Regular meditation hones the ability to sustain focus and concentration. This heightened attentiveness can extend to various aspects of life, enabling individuals to engage more fully in their daily activities and relationships.

Opening the Heart Centre

Loving-kindness meditation, another mindfulness practice, involves directing feelings of love and goodwill toward oneself and others. This practice opens the heart centre, promoting emotional resilience, empathy, and a sense of interconnectedness with all living beings.

Transcending Dualities

Meditation and mindfulness help individuals transcend dualistic thinking—moving beyond concepts of good and bad, right and wrong. This shift in perspective encourages a more holistic understanding of life, fostering spiritual growth.

Spiritual Insight and Intuition

Meditation is a fertile ground for receiving spiritual insights and developing intuition. By quieting the mind and creating inner stillness, individuals may access a deeper wisdom that goes beyond rational thinking, contributing to their spiritual evolution.

Living Mindfully

Mindfulness is not confined to formal meditation sessions; it extends to daily life. Bringing mindfulness into everyday activities—eating, walking, working—helps individuals live more intentionally and authentically, promoting spiritual growth in the midst of ordinary experiences.

Integration into Daily Life

Both meditation and mindfulness are tools for integrating spiritual principles into daily life. The insights gained during practice can guide individuals in making conscious and aligned choices, fostering a harmonious integration of the spiritual and material realms.

Ongoing Practice

Spiritual growth is a continuous journey, and meditation and mindfulness are ongoing practices. Consistent engagement with these tools deepens their impact, contributing to sustained self-discovery, inner peace, and the unfolding of one's spiritual path.

In essence, meditation and mindfulness are not only techniques but profound gateways to the soul. They provide the means to explore the inner landscape, cultivate presence, and foster a conscious and awakened way of being in the world—essential elements for those on a journey of spiritual growth.

Foundations of Meditation

Explore the Historical and Cultural Roots of Meditation

Meditation has a rich and diverse history rooted in various cultural and religious traditions. Its practice spans thousands of years and has evolved in different forms across the globe. Here's an exploration of the historical and cultural roots of meditation:

Ancient India

The origins of meditation can be traced back to ancient India, where it is deeply ingrained in the spiritual and philosophical traditions. The earliest written records on meditation are found in the Vedas, ancient Hindu scriptures dating back over 3,000 years. The Upanishads, which are philosophical texts associated with the Vedas, discuss contemplative practices aimed at understanding the nature of the self (Atman) and the ultimate reality (Brahman).

Vedic Period (1500–500 BCE)

During the Vedic period, meditation practices were formalised, and the concept of 'Dhyana' (meditation) emerged as a systematic discipline. The earliest recorded meditation techniques were part of the Vedic sacrificial rituals, where priests engaged in deep contemplation to connect with cosmic forces.

Buddhist Meditation (6th century BCE)

Siddhartha Gautama, later known as the Buddha, played a crucial role in popularising meditation. After attaining enlightenment, the Buddha developed various meditation techniques, including mindfulness and concentration practices. These techniques formed the foundation of Buddhist meditation, spreading across Asia as Buddhism expanded.

Taoist Meditation (4th–3rd century BCE)

In ancient China, Taoist philosophy introduced meditation as a means of achieving harmony with the Tao, the fundamental force underlying all existence. Taoist meditation practices, including Qigong and Dao Yin, focused on cultivating life energy (Qi) and achieving balance within the body and the natural world.

Judaism and Christian Mysticism

Meditation also has roots in Judaic and Christian mysticism. Practices such as Jewish Kabbalistic meditation and Christian contemplative prayer emerged to deepen the connection with the divine. Figures like the Desert Fathers in early Christian monasticism engaged in contemplative practices.

Islamic Sufism

Sufism, the mystical tradition within Islam, incorporates meditation as a means of achieving spiritual closeness to Allah. Sufi practitioners engage in various forms of dhikr (remembrance of God) and meditation to attain a heightened state of consciousness and divine union.

Ancient Greece and Hellenistic Period (6th–4th century BCE)

Greek philosophers, including Pythagoras and Plato, explored contemplative practices aimed at understanding the nature of the self and the cosmos. The term 'meditation' itself is derived from the Latin word 'meditation,' which translates to contemplation.

Japanese Zen Buddhism (7th century CE)

Zen Buddhism, originating in China and later flourishing in Japan, emphasises seated meditation (Zazen) as a direct path to enlightenment. Zen meditation became a central practice in monastic settings and influenced various aspects of Japanese culture, including tea ceremonies and martial arts.

Indigenous Traditions

Many indigenous cultures worldwide have traditional forms of meditation or contemplative practices deeply integrated into their spiritual rituals. These practices often involve connecting with nature, ancestors, and the spiritual dimensions of the world.

Contemporary Global Practices

Today, meditation has transcended its cultural and religious origins, becoming a global phenomenon. Various forms of meditation, including mindfulness, transcendental meditation, and loving-kindness meditation, are practiced by people worldwide for purposes ranging from stress reduction to spiritual growth.

In summary, the historical and cultural roots of meditation are diverse and interconnected, reflecting the human quest for spiritual understanding, inner peace, and connection with the divine. Through millennia, different cultures and traditions have developed unique approaches to meditation, contributing to the rich tapestry of contemplative practices observed globally today.

Define Meditation and Its Various Forms Across Different Traditions.

Meditation is a diverse set of practices that involve training the mind and cultivating a state of focused attention, heightened awareness, or deep relaxation. While the specific techniques and purposes of meditation can vary widely across different traditions, the fundamental goal is often to achieve mental clarity, emotional balance, and spiritual insight. Here are some definitions and examples of meditation across various traditions:

Hindu Meditation

In Hinduism, meditation is often referred to as 'Dhyana.' It is a central component of the yogic path, with practices like concentration on a single point (Dharana) leading to meditation and ultimately to absorption (Samadhi). Transcendental Meditation (TM) is a modern form of Hindu meditation that gained popularity in the West.

Buddhist Meditation

Buddhism incorporates various forms of meditation, with mindfulness (Vipassana) and concentration (Samatha) being fundamental. Insight meditation (Vipassana) aims at observing thoughts and sensations to gain insight into the nature of reality. Zen Buddhism emphasises seated meditation (Zazen), while Tibetan Buddhism utilises practices like analytical meditation.

Taoist Meditation

Taoist meditation aims at aligning the individual with the Tao, the fundamental force of existence. Practices include Qigong and Dao Yin, which involve movement, breath control, and visualisation to harmonise the flow of life energy (Qi) in the body.

Judaic and Christian Meditation

In Judaic and Christian traditions, meditation takes various forms, such as contemplative prayer, lectio divina, and centreing prayer. These practices involve silent reflection, repetition of sacred texts, and cultivating a receptive attitude toward divine presence.

Islamic Sufi Meditation

Sufi mysticism incorporates meditation as a means of achieving closeness to Allah. Dhikr, or the remembrance of God, involves repetitive chanting of divine names or phrases. Sufi orders also engage in various forms of meditation to attain spiritual insights and connection.

Ancient Greek Philosophy

Greek philosophers, including Pythagoras and Plato, explored contemplative practices aimed at understanding the nature of the self and the cosmos. These practices involved introspection, intellectual inquiry, and philosophical dialogue.

Japanese Zen Meditation

Zen Buddhism, with its emphasis on direct experience and enlightenment, practices seated meditation (Zazen). Zazen involves sitting in a specific posture, focusing on the breath, and observing thoughts without attachment. The aim is to experience a direct perception of reality.

Indigenous Meditation Practices

Indigenous cultures worldwide have traditional contemplative practices often integrated into spiritual rituals. These practices may involve connecting with nature, engaging in vision quests, or using dance and chanting to reach altered states of consciousness.

Loving-Kindness Meditation (Metta)

Found in both Buddhist and non-Buddhist traditions, loving-kindness meditation involves cultivating feelings of love and compassion toward oneself and others. Practitioners extend well-wishes and goodwill to individuals, gradually expanding to include all sentient beings.

Guided Meditation

In guided meditation, a teacher or recording leads participants through a specific visualisation or narrative to evoke relaxation, inner exploration, or healing. This form of meditation is commonly used in therapeutic and mindfulness settings.

These examples highlight the diversity of meditation practices across various traditions. While techniques may differ, the common thread is the intentional cultivation of a focused, aware, and often transcendent state of mind for personal and spiritual development.

Mind-Body Connection

Examine the Scientific Understanding of the Mind-body Connection in the Context of Meditation.

The mind-body connection is a complex and dynamic interrelationship between mental and physical health. Scientific research has increasingly explored how practices like meditation impact this connection, shedding light on the physiological and psychological mechanisms involved. Here is an examination of the scientific understanding of the mind-body connection in the context of meditation:

Neuroplasticity

Meditation has been linked to changes in brain structure and function, a phenomenon known as neuroplasticity. Studies using neuroimaging techniques like fMRI and EEG have shown alterations in brain regions associated with attention, memory, and emotional regulation among regular meditators. These changes suggest that the mind's training through meditation can influence the physical structure and function of the brain.

Stress Response and Cortisol Levels

Chronic stress can negatively impact physical health. Meditation, particularly mindfulness-based practices, has been shown to modulate the body's stress response. Studies indicate reductions in cortisol levels, a hormone associated with stress, in individuals who engage in regular meditation. This suggests that meditation may contribute to a healthier stress response and mitigate the negative effects of chronic stress on the body.

Immune System Function

There is evidence suggesting that meditation practices may influence the immune system. Mindfulness meditation, for example, has been associated with changes in immune function markers. Studies indicate potential improvements in immune response and a reduction in markers of inflammation, suggesting a link between meditation and enhanced immune system function.

Cardiovascular Health

Meditation has been linked to improvements in cardiovascular health. Research shows that meditation practices, including mindfulness and transcendental meditation, may contribute to reduced blood pressure, improved heart rate variability, and enhanced overall cardiovascular function. These effects are crucial for long-term heart health and the prevention of cardiovascular diseases.

Pain Perception and Management

Meditation has been explored as a complementary approach to pain management. Mindfulness meditation, in particular, has been associated with changes in pain perception and increased pain tolerance. Brain imaging studies suggest that meditation may influence the brain's pain-processing centres, providing insights into the mind's ability to modulate the experience of pain.

Emotional Regulation

The mind-body connection is closely tied to emotional regulation. Meditation practices, especially those emphasising mindfulness, have been shown to enhance emotional regulation by promoting awareness and acceptance of emotions. Neuroimaging studies suggest changes in brain regions associated with emotional processing, indicating the impact of meditation on emotional well-being.

Epigenetic Changes

Some studies suggest that meditation practices may lead to epigenetic changes—modifications in gene expression without altering the underlying DNA sequence. This highlights the potential for meditation to influence biological processes at a molecular level, showcasing the intricate interplay between mental and physical health.

Brain Wave Patterns

Meditation has been associated with changes in brain wave patterns, including increased theta and alpha waves. These patterns are linked to states of relaxation, focused attention, and altered states of consciousness. Understanding these neurophysiological changes provides insights into how meditation influences the mind's states and the body's responses.

Mind-Body Interventions in Healthcare

The scientific understanding of the mind-body connection has led to the integration of mind-body interventions, including meditation, into healthcare settings. Meditation-based programmes are increasingly recognised as valuable components of comprehensive healthcare strategies, addressing both mental and physical aspects of well-being.

In conclusion, the scientific exploration of meditation's impact on the mind-body connection has revealed a multitude of interconnected effects, spanning from neuroplasticity to immune function and emotional regulation. These findings underscore the intricate relationship between mental and physical health, emphasising the potential of meditation as a tool for promoting holistic well-being. Continued research in this field holds promise for uncovering further insights into the mechanisms through which meditation influences the mind-body connection.

Discuss the Impact of Meditation on Brain Function, Stress Response, and Overall Well-being

Meditation has been the subject of extensive scientific research, and the evidence suggests a positive impact on brain function, stress response, and overall well-being. Here's a discussion of these effects:

Attention and Cognitive Function

Enhanced Attention and Concentration: Meditation practices often involve focusing attention on a particular object, thought, or breath. This sustained focus can lead to improvements in attention and concentration, as observed in studies using tasks that measure cognitive performance.

Changes in Brain Wave Patterns: Meditation has been associated with alterations in brain wave patterns, including increased theta and alpha waves. These patterns are linked to states of relaxation, focused attention, and improved cognitive function.

Sleep Improvement

Promotion of Better Sleep: Regular meditation has been linked to improvements in sleep quality. Mindfulness meditation, in particular, may help individuals manage insomnia and other sleep disorders by promoting relaxation and reducing stress-related factors that contribute to sleep disturbances.

Mind-Body Connection

Enhanced Mind-Body Connection: Meditation encourages a heightened awareness of the mind-body connection. Practices such as body scan meditations involve consciously directing attention to various parts of the body, fostering a greater understanding of bodily sensations and promoting overall well-being.

Blood Pressure and Cardiovascular Health

Blood Pressure Regulation: Meditation has been associated with reductions in blood pressure, which is a crucial factor in cardiovascular health. Studies suggest that meditation practices can contribute to lower blood pressure levels and improved heart rate variability.

Cardiovascular Disease Prevention: Due to its positive impact on stress reduction and blood pressure regulation, meditation may play a role in preventing cardiovascular diseases and promoting heart health.

Overall Well-Being and Quality of Life

Enhanced Quality of Life: Regular meditation has been linked to an enhanced sense of well-being and an improved quality of life. Practitioners often report increased life satisfaction, a greater sense of purpose, and improved overall happiness.

In conclusion, the impact of meditation on brain function, stress response, and overall well-being is supported by a growing body of scientific research. These positive effects underscore the potential of meditation as a valuable tool for promoting mental and physical health, with applications ranging from stress management to the prevention and treatment of various health conditions. Continued research is likely to provide further insights into the nuanced ways in which meditation influences the mind and body.

Types of Meditation Practices

Introduce Different Meditation Techniques, Such As Mindfulness Meditation, Loving-kindness Meditation, and Transcendental Meditation

Meditation is a diverse practice, and various techniques cater to different goals and preferences. Here's an introduction to three distinct meditation techniques: mindfulness meditation, loving-kindness meditation, and transcendental meditation.

Mindfulness Meditation

Overview: Mindfulness meditation is rooted in Buddhist traditions and has gained widespread popularity in secular contexts. It involves cultivating a heightened awareness of the present-moment and observing thoughts and sensations without judgement.

Technique

- Find a quiet space and assume a comfortable posture, either sitting or lying down.
- Focus your attention on the breath, sensations in the body, or an anchor point like a mantra.
- When the mind wanders (as it inevitably will), gently bring your focus back to the chosen point without self-judgement.
- This practice encourages non-reactive awareness and acceptance of the present-moment.

Loving-Kindness Meditation (Metta)

Overview: Also rooted in Buddhist traditions, loving-kindness meditation, or Metta, aims to cultivate feelings of love and compassion towards oneself and others.

It fosters a sense of connection and well-wishing for all beings.

Technique

- Begin in a comfortable meditation posture, focusing on your breath to establish a calm state.
- Direct positive intentions and phrases (e.g., "May you/I be happy, may you/I be healthy") towards yourself.
- Gradually extend these intentions to loved ones, acquaintances, and eventually to all beings.
- The practice aims to nurture a genuine sense of love and compassion, breaking down barriers and promoting a positive mindset.

Transcendental Meditation (TM)

Overview: Transcendental Meditation is a mantra-based technique that originated in ancient Vedic traditions. TM is known for its simplicity and accessibility.

Technique

- Sit comfortably with closed eyes for 20 minutes twice a day.

- Repeat a specific mantra silently in the mind.
- When thoughts arise, gently return to the mantra without effort.
- TM aims to lead the practitioner to a state of restful alertness, transcending ordinary thought and promoting deep relaxation.

Each of these meditation techniques offers unique benefits and appeals to different individuals based on their goals and preferences. Mindfulness meditation enhances present-moment awareness, loving-kindness meditation fosters compassion and connection, and transcendental meditation aims to achieve a state of deep rest and relaxation. Exploring various techniques allows individuals to find the one that resonates most with them and aligns with their specific needs and objectives.

Provide Guidance on Choosing the Right Meditation Practice for Individual Preferences and Goals

Choosing the right meditation practice involves considering your individual preferences, goals, and lifestyle. Here are some guidelines to help you select a meditation practice that aligns with your needs:

Clarify Your Goals

Stress Reduction: If your primary goal is stress reduction and relaxation, practices like mindfulness meditation, body scan meditation, or transcendental meditation may be beneficial.

Emotional Well-Being: For enhancing emotional well-being and cultivating positive emotions, loving-kindness meditation (Metta) or other compassion-based practices are suitable.

Improved Focus and Concentration: If you are seeking to enhance focus and concentration, mindfulness meditation or concentration meditation, focusing on a specific point or object, may be effective.

Consider Your Personality and Preferences

Active vs. Passive: If you prefer an active approach, consider movement-based meditations like walking meditation or yoga. If you prefer a more passive approach, seated meditation practices may be suitable.

Guided vs. Silent: Some individuals find guided meditations helpful, providing instructions and prompts. Others may prefer silent meditation, allowing space for self-directed practice.

Explore Different Traditions

Secular vs. Spiritual: Determine whether you are more comfortable with a secular or spiritual approach. Mindfulness meditation is often presented in a secular context, while practices like loving-kindness meditation have spiritual roots.

Cultural Considerations: Some meditation practices have cultural or religious origins. Explore practices aligned with your cultural background or those that resonate with you personally.

Assess Lifestyle and Schedule

Time Commitment: Consider the amount of time you can realistically commit to meditation each day. Practices like mindfulness meditation and loving-kindness meditation can be adapted to fit shorter or longer time frames.

Consistency: Choose a practice that fits your daily routine. Consistency is often more important than duration, so opt for a practice that you can integrate seamlessly into your life.

Try Different Techniques

Experiment: Attend meditation classes, workshops, or use meditation apps to explore different techniques.

Trying various practices helps you discover what resonates with you and what feels most comfortable.

Reflect on Experiences: After trying different techniques, reflect on your experiences. Note which practices bring a sense of calm, fulfilment, or alignment with your goals.

Seek Professional Guidance

Mentor or Teacher: Consider seeking guidance from a meditation teacher or mentor, especially when exploring practices with specific cultural or spiritual contexts. They can offer personalised advice and support.

Be Open to Adaptation

Evolve with Your Needs: As your goals and circumstances change, be open to adapting your meditation practice. What works for you today may evolve over time.

Listen to Your Intuition

Trust Yourself: Ultimately, trust your intuition. Choose a meditation practice that feels right for you, even if it doesn't conform to popular trends or recommendations.

Remember that there is no one-size-fits-all approach to meditation. The key is to find a practice that resonates with you, aligns with your goals, and can be seamlessly integrated into your life. Regular and sincere practice, regardless of the specific technique, is often the most significant factor in experiencing the benefits of meditation.

Mindfulness in Everyday Life

Discuss the Integration of Mindfulness into Daily Activities and Routines

Integrating mindfulness into daily activities and routines is a powerful way to cultivate present-moment awareness and promote a sense of calm and focus throughout the day. Mindfulness is not limited to formal meditation sessions; it can become a way of life. Here are some strategies for incorporating mindfulness into your daily activities:

Mindful Breathing

During Daily Tasks, Incorporate conscious breathing into routine activities such as commuting, washing dishes, or waiting in line. Pay attention to your breath, inhaling and exhaling mindfully, bringing your focus to the present-moment.

Mindful Eating

Savour Each Bite When eating, take your time to savour each bite. Notice the flavours, textures, and sensations.

Put away distractions like phones or screens and focus solely on the act of eating.

Mindful Walking

Conscious Steps: Whether walking to work, taking a stroll, or moving from one room to another, pay attention to each step. Feel the connection of your feet with the ground and the movement of your body.

Mindful Listening

Fully Engage: When engaging in conversations, practice mindful listening. Give your full attention to the speaker, resist the urge to formulate responses while they're talking, and be present with the words and emotions being shared.

Mindful Work

Single-Tasking While working, focus on one task at a time. Avoid multitasking and bring your attention fully to the current activity. Take short breaks to practice mindful breathing or stretching.

Mindful Driving

Drive with Awareness While driving, pay attention to the sensations of steering, the movement of the vehicle, and the environment around you. Minimise distractions and be fully present on the road.

Mindful Technology Use

Set Boundaries Establish specific times for checking emails or using social media. When engaging with technology, do so with intentionality and awareness, avoiding mindless scrolling or constant checking.

Mindful Pause

Take Breaks: Incorporate short mindfulness breaks throughout the day. Set alarms or reminders to pause, breathe, and bring your attention back to the present. This can be especially beneficial during hectic or stressful moments.

Mindful Hygiene

Conscious Self-Care: While showering, brushing your teeth, or engaging in other self-care activities, bring your attention to the sensations and movements involved. Use these moments as opportunities for mindful presence.

Mindful Environment Awareness

Observe Your Surroundings Periodically, pause and observe your environment. Notice the colours, shapes, and sounds around you. Ground yourself in the present-moment by connecting with the sensory experience of your surroundings.

Mindful Gratitude

Reflect on Blessings Take a moment each day to reflect on things you are grateful for. It could be as simple as acknowledging the warmth of sunlight or expressing gratitude for relationships and opportunities. Mindful Reflection

End-of-Day Review Before bedtime, reflect on your day without judgement. Acknowledge both challenges and moments of joy. This reflective practice can help you gain insight and foster a sense of closure.

Remember that mindfulness is about cultivating awareness and being fully present in the current moment. Start by incorporating one or two of these practices into your routine, gradually expanding as you feel more comfortable. Over time, mindfulness can become a natural and integrated part of your daily life, contributing to overall well-being and a greater sense of peace.

Explore How Mindfulness Can Enhance Awareness and Presence in Everyday Experiences

Mindfulness, at its core, is the practice of bringing intentional and non-judgemental awareness to the present-moment. When integrated into everyday experiences, mindfulness enhances awareness and presence in profound ways. Here's an exploration of how mindfulness contributes to heightened awareness and presence in various aspects of daily life:

Mindful Breathing

Awareness of the Breath Mindfulness often begins with a focus on the breath. By paying attention to the inhalation and exhalation, individuals anchor themselves in the present-moment, cultivating a heightened awareness of the breath's rhythm and sensations.

Mindful Eating

Savouring the Experience Mindful eating involves fully engaging in the act of eating. It encourages individuals to savour each bite, paying attention to the flavours, textures, and smells. This heightened awareness fosters a deeper connection with the act of nourishing the body.

Mindful Walking

Feeling Each Step Whether walking in nature or moving within the confines of a space, mindfulness in walking involves feeling each step consciously. The sensations of the feet lifting, moving, and making contact with the ground become a focal point, grounding the individual in the present-moment.

Mindful Listening

Full Engagement in Conversations: Mindful listening entails giving one's full attention to the speaker. It involves not only hearing the words but also being attuned to the speaker's emotions, tone, and body language. This practice deepens connections and enriches communication.

Mindful Work

Present-Moment Focus Mindfulness at work involves focusing on one task at a time, fully immersing oneself in the present activity. This promotes a state of flow, where time seems to pass effortlessly, and the quality of work improves.

Mindful Driving

Attentive Awareness on the Road While driving, mindfulness encourages individuals to be fully present on the road. This involves observing the environment, feeling the steering and movements of the vehicle, and resisting distractions to ensure safe and aware driving.

Mindful Technology Use

Engagement Mindfulness Intentional with technology involves conscious and intentional use. It encourages individuals to notice their impulses to check devices mindlessly, set boundaries for technology use, and engage with screens with full awareness.

Mindful Pause

Taking Breath Breaks Incorporating short mindful breaks throughout the day allows individuals to pause, breathe, and centre themselves. This practice can be especially helpful during busy or stressful periods, fostering a sense of calm and clarity.

Mindful Hygiene

Sensory Awareness Routine activities like showering, brushing teeth, or grooming become opportunities for sensory awareness. Feeling the water, the movement of the body, and the texture of products can transform these moments into mindful experiences.

Mindful Environment Awareness

Observing Surroundings Practicing mindfulness involves periodically stopping to observe one's environment. This can include noticing the colours, shapes, and sounds around and fostering a connection with the present-moment.

Mindful Gratitude

Reflecting on Blessings Incorporating mindfulness into gratitude practices involves reflecting on and appreciating the positive aspects of life. This intentional acknowledgement of blessings enhances awareness of the richness present in everyday experiences.

Mindful Reflection

End-of-Day Review Mindfulness extends to reflective practices at the end of the day. Without judgement, individuals can review their experiences, acknowledging challenges and moments of joy, contributing to a sense of self-awareness.

By weaving mindfulness into these everyday experiences, individuals cultivate a state of heightened awareness, fostering a deeper connection with the richness of each moment. This intentional presence contributes to a more fulfilling and grounded experience of daily life.

Health Benefits of Meditation

Examine the Physical and Mental Health Benefits Associated With Regular Meditation Practice

Regular meditation practice has been linked to a wide range of physical and mental health benefits. These benefits are supported by a growing body of scientific research and are increasingly recognised by healthcare professionals. Here's an examination of the notable physical and mental health benefits associated with regular meditation:

Physical Health Benefits:

Stress Reduction

Cortisol Regulation Meditation has been shown to reduce cortisol levels, the hormone associated with stress. Regular practice helps the body's stress response become more adaptive, leading to lower overall stress levels.

Cardiovascular Health

Blood Pressure Regulation Various forms of meditation, including mindfulness and transcendental meditation, have been linked to lower blood pressure. This contributes to improved cardiovascular health and a reduced risk of heart diseases.

Immune System Support

Enhanced Immune Function Meditation may positively impact the immune system, with studies suggesting improvements in immune response and a reduction in inflammation markers. A robust immune system is crucial for overall health and disease prevention.

Pain Management

Increased Pain Tolerance Meditation, particularly mindfulness-based practices, has been associated with increased pain tolerance and decreased perception of pain. This can be beneficial for individuals dealing with chronic pain conditions.

Improved Sleep

Sleep Quality Regular meditation has been shown to improve sleep quality. Mindfulness meditation and relaxation techniques help calm the mind, making it easier for individuals to fall asleep and experience more restful sleep.

Enhanced Respiratory Function

Improved Breathing Meditation often involves focused attention on the breath, leading to improved respiratory function. This can be particularly beneficial for individuals with respiratory conditions such as asthma.

Hormonal Balance

Endocrine System Regulation Regular meditation may contribute to the regulation of the endocrine system, including the balance of hormones. This has implications for various bodily functions, including metabolism and mood regulation.

Mental Health Benefits:

Stress and Anxiety Reduction

Mindfulness-Based Stress Reduction (MBSR) Mindfulness meditation, as incorporated in MBSR programmes, has proven effective in reducing symptoms of stress and anxiety. It helps individuals develop a non-reactive awareness of their thoughts and emotions.

Depression Management

Mindfulness-Based Cognitive Therapy (MBCT) MBCT, which integrates mindfulness with cognitive therapy, has been shown to be effective in preventing the recurrence of depression. Meditation helps individuals become more aware of negative thought patterns and break the cycle of depressive relapse.

Improved Emotional Regulation

Greater Emotional Resilience Meditation practices, especially those focused on mindfulness, contribute to improved emotional regulation. Practitioners develop the ability to observe emotions without being overwhelmed, fostering emotional resilience.

Enhanced Concentration and Cognitive Function

Increased Attention Span Meditation practices, such as focused attention meditation, have been associated with improvements in attention and concentration. This is beneficial for cognitive tasks that require sustained focus.

Memory Improvement

Better Working Memory Meditation has been linked to improvements in working memory, the system responsible for temporarily holding and manipulating information. This can contribute to better cognitive performance.

Mind-Wandering Reduction

Less Distracted Thinking Meditation practices, particularly those that involve focused attention, help reduce mind-wandering and improve the ability to stay present in the moment. This has positive implications for task efficiency and productivity.

Positive Changes in Brain Structure

- *Neuroplasticity:* Meditation has been associated with changes in brain structure and function, particularly in areas related to self-awareness, empathy, and emotional regulation. This phenomenon, known as neuroplasticity, reflects the brain's ability to adapt and reorganise.

Increased Well-Being and Life Satisfaction

- *Subjective Well-Being:* Regular meditation has been linked to increased subjective well-being and life satisfaction. Practitioners often report a greater sense of purpose, happiness, and fulfilment in their lives.

Overall Quality of Life:

1. **Mind-Body Connection:**

   – *Holistic Well-Being:* Meditation encourages a strong mind-body connection, fostering an overall sense of well-being. This integrated approach contributes to a healthier and more balanced lifestyle.

2. **Resilience to Stressors:**

   – *Coping Mechanisms:* Through mindfulness and self-awareness, meditation equips individuals with effective coping mechanisms to deal with life's challenges. This resilience to stressors contributes to mental and emotional well-being.

3. **Enhanced Self-Awareness:**

   – *Greater Understanding of Self:* Regular meditation encourages self-reflection and self-awareness. This deeper understanding of oneself contributes to personal growth and the development of a more authentic and fulfilling life.

4. **Improved Interpersonal Relationships:**

   - *Increased Empathy and Compassion:* Meditation practices, including loving-kindness meditation, foster qualities such as empathy and compassion. This positively influences interpersonal relationships, promoting understanding and connection.

In summary, the physical and mental health benefits associated with regular meditation are extensive and well-documented. From stress reduction and improved cardiovascular health to enhanced emotional regulation and overall well-being, the holistic impact of meditation makes it a valuable tool for promoting a healthier and more balanced life. Incorporating meditation into a daily routine can lead to long-term positive effects on both physical and mental health.

Meditation and Emotional Regulation

Explore How Meditation Can Be a Powerful Tool for Managing and Regulating Emotions.

Meditation serves as a powerful tool for managing and regulating emotions by fostering self-awareness, enhancing emotional intelligence, and promoting a more skillful response to various emotional states. Here's an exploration of how meditation contributes to emotional well-being:

1. **Increased Self-Awareness:**

   – *Mindful Observation:* Meditation encourages individuals to observe their thoughts and emotions without judgement. This mindful observation cultivates heightened self-awareness, enabling individuals to recognise and understand their emotional states.

2. **Emotional Acceptance:**

   – *Non-Judgemental Awareness:* Meditation practices, especially those rooted in mindfulness, promote non-judgemental awareness of emotions. By accepting emotions without attaching labels of 'good' or 'bad,' individuals can create a healthier relationship with their emotional experiences.

3. **Enhanced Emotional Regulation:**

   – *Focused Attention:* Techniques such as focused attention meditation involve directing attention to a specific object or breath. This focused attention enhances the ability to regulate emotions by creating a mental space between the individual and their emotional reactions.

4. **Mindfulness-Based Stress Reduction (MBSR):**

   – *Cultivating Presence:* MBSR programmes incorporate mindfulness meditation to cultivate present-moment awareness. This presence enables individuals to respond more skillfully to stressors, reducing the likelihood of impulsive emotional reactions.

5. **Loving-Kindness Meditation (Metta):**

   – Cultivating Compassion: Metta meditation involves generating feelings of love and compassion towards oneself and others. This practice fosters a positive emotional state, enhances empathy, and contributes to more compassionate responses in daily life.

6. **Reduced Emotional Reactivity:**

   – *Mindful Response vs. Reaction:* Meditation helps individuals move from reactive responses to more mindful and intentional reactions. By cultivating a pause between stimulus and response, individuals gain the ability to choose their emotional responses consciously.

7. **Emotion Regulation Networks in the Brain:**

   – *Neuroplasticity:* Meditation has been associated with neuroplastic changes in the brain, particularly in areas related to emotional regulation. Regular practice strengthens neural pathways associated with self-control and emotional resilience.

8. **Mindfulness-Based Cognitive Therapy (MBCT):**

   – *Breaking Negative Thought Patterns:* MBCT combines mindfulness with cognitive therapy to address negative thought patterns associated with emotions like depression. By becoming aware of these patterns, individuals can interrupt and reframe them, leading to improved emotional well-being.

9. **Enhanced Emotional Resilience:**

   – *Stress Reduction:* Through practices such as deep breathing or body scan meditation, individuals can activate the body's relaxation response, reducing stress and promoting emotional resilience in the face of challenges.

10. **Greater Emotional Flexibility:**

    – *Open Awareness:* Meditation encourages open awareness, allowing individuals to hold space for a wide range of emotions.

This flexibility helps in navigating complex emotional landscapes without feeling overwhelmed.

11. **Improved Interpersonal Relationships:**

    – *Empathy and Connection:* Loving-kindness meditation and compassion-focused practices enhance empathy and connection with others. By understanding and regulating one's own emotions, individuals can also relate more empathetically to the emotions of others.

12. **Mindful Breathing for Emotional Calmness:**

    – *Calm Abiding:* Mindful breathing exercises, where attention is focused on the breath, promote emotional calmness. This practice can be particularly effective in managing intense emotions and preventing emotional overwhelm.

In summary, meditation serves as a potent tool for managing and regulating emotions by promoting self-awareness, cultivating emotional intelligence, and providing practical strategies for responding to various emotional states. Through regular practice, individuals can develop a more balanced and skillful approach to their emotions, ultimately leading to enhanced emotional well-being.

Provide Practical Techniques for Using Meditation to Cultivate Emotional Resilience.

Cultivating emotional resilience through meditation involves developing skills to navigate and bounce back from challenging emotions. Here are practical meditation techniques that can help enhance emotional resilience:

1. **Mindful Breathing:**

   - *Technique:* Find a comfortable seated position. Focus your attention on your breath, observing each inhalation and exhalation. When distractions arise, gently bring your focus back to the breath.

   - *Benefits:* Mindful breathing promotes awareness of the present-moment, creating a mental space to observe and respond to emotions with greater clarity and calmness.

2. **Loving-Kindness Meditation (Metta):**

   - *Technique:* Sit comfortably and extend feelings of love and goodwill towards yourself and others. Start with phrases like

"May I be happy, may I be healthy," and gradually expand to include loved ones, acquaintances, and even those with whom you may have challenges.

- *Benefits:* Metta meditation fosters compassion, empathy, and a positive emotional state, contributing to resilience in the face of adversity.

3. **Body Scan Meditation:**
   - *Technique:* Lie down or sit comfortably. Direct your attention to different parts of your body, observing sensations without judgement. Progressively move through each body part, from toes to head.
   - *Benefits:* Body scan meditation enhances body-mind awareness, helping individuals recognise and release physical tension associated with emotional stress.

4. **Mindful Walking:**
   - *Technique:* Walk slowly and deliberately, paying attention to each step. Feel the connection between your feet and the ground. Notice the sensations in your body as you move.

- *Benefits:* Mindful walking provides a grounding practice, promoting present-moment awareness and easing the mind during times of emotional turbulence.

5. **Breath Awareness in Difficult Moments:**

   - *Technique:* In challenging situations, take a few moments to focus on your breath. Inhale deeply, exhale slowly. This simple practice can be done discreetly and helps calm the nervous system.

   - *Benefits:* Using breath awareness as a quick intervention in difficult moments aids in emotional regulation, preventing impulsive reactions.

6. **Gratitude Meditation:**

   - *Technique:* Sit comfortably and reflect on things you are grateful for. Focus on the positive aspects of your life, expressing gratitude for people, experiences, or qualities.

   - *Benefits:* Gratitude meditation shifts focus to positive aspects, fostering a resilient mindset that can better withstand challenges.

7. **Mindful Observation of Thoughts:**

   – *Technique:* Sit in meditation and observe your thoughts without getting entangled in them. Acknowledge thoughts as they arise, allowing them to pass without attachment.

   – *Benefits:* Developing a non-judgemental awareness of thoughts helps create distance from negative patterns, contributing to emotional resilience.

8. **R.A.I.N. Technique (Recognise, Allow, Investigate, Nurture):**

   - *Technique:* When facing difficult emotions, apply the R.A.I.N. technique. Recognise the emotion, allow it to be present without resistance, investigate the sensations and thoughts associated with it, and nurture yourself with self-compassion.

   – *Benefits:* R.A.I.N. provides a structured approach to handling intense emotions, promoting understanding and self-compassion.

9. **Guided Imagery Meditation:**

   – *Technique:* Close your eyes and visualise a calming or empowering scenario. Engage your senses in the imagined experience, focusing on the details.

- *Benefits:* Guided imagery helps create a mental sanctuary, providing a refuge during stressful times and fostering emotional resilience.

10. Breath Counting:

- *Technique:* Inhale deeply, exhale, and count each breath cycle. Start with one and continue to ten, then start again. If the mind wanders, gently return to counting.
- *Benefits:* Breath counting enhances concentration and focus, supporting emotional resilience by training the mind to remain centred.

Incorporating these meditation techniques into regular practice can contribute to the development of emotional resilience. Consistency is key, and over time, these practices can become valuable tools for navigating life's challenges with greater ease and equanimity.

Guided Meditation Practices

Include Step-by-step Guided Meditation Scripts for Readers to Follow

Certainly! Below are two guided meditation scripts—one for mindfulness breathing and another for loving-kindness (Metta) meditation. These scripts are designed to help you cultivate emotional resilience through focused awareness and positive intentions.

Mindfulness Breathing Meditation:

Introduction

Begin by finding a comfortable seated position. Sit with your spine straight and your hands resting on your lap or knees. Close your eyes gently. Take a moment to settle into your breath.

Body Awareness

Bring your attention to the sensations in your body. Notice the points of contact between your body and the chair or floor. Feel the weight of your body grounding you in the present-moment.

Inhalation and Exhalation

Shift your focus to your breath. Observe each inhalation and exhalation. Notice the rise and fall of your chest or the sensation of the breath entering and leaving your nostrils.

Counting the Breaths

As you breathe in, silently count 'one.' As you breathe out, count 'two.' Continue counting each breath up to ten, and then start again at one. If your mind wanders, gently bring it back to the count.

Expanding Awareness

Expand your awareness to include the entire breath cycle. Notice the pause between the inhalation and exhalation. Allow each breath to be a full, mindful experience.

Dealing with Distractions

If your mind becomes distracted, acknowledge it without judgement and gently guide your attention back to the breath. Use the breath as an anchor to bring you back to the present-moment.

Closing

As we conclude, take a few deep breaths. Feel a sense of gratitude for this moment of mindfulness. When you are ready, gently open your eyes.

Introduction

Sit in a comfortable position, allowing your body to relax. Close your eyes and take a few deep breaths. Bring your attention to the present-moment.

Setting Positive Intentions

Begin by setting a positive intention for your practice. This could be a wish for your own well-being, the well-being of others, or a broader sense of peace in the world.

Self-Love and Compassion

Direct your focus inward and extend warm wishes to yourself. Silently repeat phrases such as "May I be happy, may I be healthy, may I be safe, may I be at ease." Allow these phrases to resonate, cultivating a sense of self-love and compassion.

Expanding Loving-Kindness

Gradually extend these wishes to others. Visualise loved ones, friends, acquaintances, and even those with whom you may have challenges. Repeat the phrases for each person, radiating loving-kindness outward.

Universal Love

Expand your loving-kindness to all beings. Envision people from different walks of life, animals, and even the Earth itself. Repeat the phrases with a sense of universal love and goodwill.

Radiating Positive Energy

Imagine a warm, radiant light emanating from your heart, carrying the energy of loving-kindness. Picture this light enveloping you and everyone around you, creating a sphere of positive energy.

Closing

As the meditation comes to an end, take a few moments to notice how you feel. When you are ready, gently open your eyes. Carry the warmth and compassion cultivated in this practice into your daily life.

Feel free to modify these scripts to suit your preferences or add personal touches. Regular practice of these guided meditations can contribute to the cultivation of emotional resilience and a greater sense of well-being.

Creating a Meditation Space

Provide Tips on Establishing a Conducive Environment for Meditation

Creating a conducive environment for meditation is essential to support a focused and peaceful practice. Here are some tips to help you establish an environment that enhances the quality of your meditation:

1. **Choose a Quiet Space:**

   – *Select a Quiet Room:* Choose a room or corner in your home that is away from noise and distractions. A quiet space helps you immerse yourself in the meditation practice without external disruptions.

2. **Set Up Comfortably:**

   – *Comfortable Seating:* Use a cushion or chair that allows you to sit comfortably with your spine straight. Ensure that your chosen seating option supports good posture without causing discomfort.

3. **Optimal Lighting:**

   – *Natural Light or Soft Lighting:* If possible, meditate in a space with natural light. Soft, diffused lighting can create a calming atmosphere. Avoid harsh, bright lights that may be distracting.

4. **Minimal Distractions:**

   – *Declutter the Space:* Remove unnecessary items from the meditation area to minimise visual distractions. Keep the space clean and organised to create a serene atmosphere.

5. **Aromatherapy:**

   – *Scented Candles or Essential Oils:* Use calming scents like lavender, chamomile, or eucalyptus to enhance relaxation. Be mindful of allergies and choose scents that are personally soothing.

6. **Comfortable Attire:**

   – *Wear Comfortable Clothing:* Dress in loose, comfortable clothing to allow for unrestricted breathing and movement. This contributes to a sense of ease during meditation.

7. **Technology-Free Zone:**

   – *Turn Off Devices:* Silence or turn off electronic devices to minimise the potential for interruptions. This includes phones, tablets, and computers.

8. **Time Management:**

   – *Allocate Dedicated Time:* Establish a consistent meditation schedule. Allocate a specific time each day for your practice, ensuring that you have enough time to settle into the meditation without feeling rushed.

9. **Mindful Decor:**

   – *Inspirational Items:* Consider adding items that inspire mindfulness, such as a small altar with meaningful objects or a calming piece of artwork. Choose items that have personal significance.

10. **Temperature Control:**

   – *Maintain a Comfortable Temperature:* Ensure the room is at a comfortable temperature, not too hot or too cold. Dress accordingly or use blankets to regulate your body temperature.

11. **Natural Elements:**

    – *Plants or Natural Elements:* Incorporate elements of nature, such as indoor plants or natural textures, to create a sense of tranquillity.

12. **Use Props if Needed:**

    – *Meditation Props:* If necessary, use props like meditation cushions or a yoga mat to enhance comfort and support during meditation.

13. **Create Rituals:**

    – *Pre-Meditation Rituals:* Establish rituals to signal the beginning of your meditation, such as lighting a candle, taking a few deep breaths, or practicing a brief grounding exercise.

14. **Respectful Environment:**

    – *Inform Others:* If you share your living space, inform family members or roommates about your meditation schedule to minimise potential disruptions.

15. **Soundscapes or Music:**

    - *Calming Sounds:* Consider playing soft instrumental music, nature sounds, or guided meditation recordings if they enhance your practice. Ensure the volume is low and non-intrusive.

16. **Posture Support:**

    - *Comfortable Meditation Posture:* If sitting on the floor is uncomfortable, use props like cushions or a meditation bench to support a comfortable and sustainable posture.

17. **Personalise the Space:**

    - Personal Touches: Add personal touches like inspirational quotes, artwork, or objects that hold sentimental value. Personalising the space can make it feel more inviting and conducive to meditation.

By implementing these tips, you can create an environment that supports a focused and enriching meditation practice. Remember that the ideal meditation space may vary from person to person, so feel free to adjust these suggestions based on your preferences and needs.

Discuss the Importance of a Dedicated Meditation Space and How to Personalise It

A dedicated meditation space holds significant importance in cultivating a consistent and deep meditation practice. Creating a personalised meditation space enhances the overall experience and encourages regularity in your mindfulness routine. Here are some reasons why a dedicated space is valuable, along with tips on how to personalise it:

Importance of a Dedicated Meditation Space:

1. **Consistency and Routine:**

   – *Psychological Cue:* Having a designated space signals to your mind that it's time for meditation. This creates a psychological cue, making it easier to transition into a meditative state consistently.

2. **Minimising Distractions:**

   – *Reduced External Interruptions:* A dedicated space minimises external distractions, allowing you to focus inward without disruptions. This is particularly important for those who share living spaces with others.

3. **Psychological Association:**

   – *Positive Associations:* Over time, your meditation space becomes associated with positive feelings of peace and tranquillity. This association strengthens the effectiveness of your meditation practice.

4. **Sacred and Intentional Atmosphere:**

   – *Spiritual Connection:* A dedicated space can have a sacred feel, fostering a sense of connection to something greater than oneself. It creates an intentional atmosphere conducive to inner exploration.

5. **Comfort and Familiarity:**

   – *Personal Comfort:* Familiarity with your meditation space enhances comfort, making it easier to let go of tension and distractions. It becomes a safe and comforting environment for self-reflection.

Overcoming Common Challenges

Address Common Challenges Faced by Individuals During Meditation, Such As Restlessness, Difficulty Focusing, or Impatience

Meditation, while immensely beneficial, can present various challenges, especially for beginners or individuals with busy minds. Addressing common challenges during meditation involves understanding that these experiences are normal and part of the process. Here are some common challenges and strategies to overcome them:

1. **Restlessness:**

   - *Challenge:* Restlessness is a common obstacle, especially for those new to meditation. It may manifest as fidgeting, a constant urge to move, or an inability to sit still.

   - *Strategy:*

- *Body Scan:* Bring attention to different parts of your body, starting from your toes and moving upward. Notice any tension and consciously release it.

- *Focused Breathing:* Redirect your focus to your breath. Concentrate on the sensations of inhaling and exhaling, grounding yourself in the present-moment.

2. **Difficulty Focusing:**

- *Challenge:* Distractions, wandering thoughts, and an inability to maintain focus are common challenges during meditation.

- *Strategy:*

- *Anchor Point:* Choose an anchor point for your attention, such as the breath, a mantra, or a specific point in your body. Whenever your mind drifts, gently guide it back to this anchor.

- *Labelling Thoughts:* Instead of getting frustrated, observe your thoughts without attachment. Label them as 'thinking' and return to your chosen focus.

3. **Impatience:**

   - *Challenge:* Impatience can arise when individuals expect immediate results or feel frustrated with the pace of their progress.

   - *Strategy:*

   - *Mindful Patience:* Acknowledge that meditation is a practice, and progress may be gradual. Cultivate a sense of mindful patience, focusing on the journey rather than the destination.

   - *Shorter Sessions:* If impatience is a significant barrier, start with shorter meditation sessions and gradually extend the duration as your practice deepens.

4. **Physical Discomfort:**

   - *Challenge:* Physical discomfort, such as stiffness or pain, can distract from the meditation experience.

   - *Strategy:*

   - *Adjust Posture:* Ensure your posture is comfortable and supported. Use props like cushions or chairs to alleviate discomfort.

- *Mindful Acceptance:* Instead of resisting discomfort, bring mindful attention to the sensations. Acknowledge them without judgement, and if needed, make gentle adjustments.

5. **Overthinking:**

   - *Challenge:* Racing thoughts, planning, or analysing during meditation can be challenging.

   - *Strategy:*

   - *Label and Release:* Label the thoughts as 'thinking' and let them go. Bring your attention back to your chosen focus, whether it's the breath or a mantra.

   - *Mindful Observation:* Observe your thoughts without getting entangled in them. Imagine them as clouds passing by, and bring your focus back to the present-moment.

6. **Fatigue or Sleepiness:**

   - *Challenge:* Feeling drowsy or sleepy during meditation sessions.

- *Strategy:*
- *Energising Techniques:* Prioritise meditation during times when you are naturally more alert. Experiment with techniques like mindful walking or slightly opening your eyes to stay awake.
- *Body Movement:* Integrate gentle stretches or movements before meditation to invigorate the body.

7. **High Expectations:**

   - *Challenge:* Setting unrealistic expectations or anticipating specific outcomes can lead to disappointment.
   - *Strategy:*
   - *Mindful Awareness:* Shift your focus from achieving specific outcomes to being present in the moment. Embrace the practice as it is, without attachment to particular results.
   - *Celebrate Small Wins:* Acknowledge and celebrate small improvements or moments of clarity during your meditation. This helps build a positive association with the practice.

8. **Inconsistency:**

   - *Challenge:* Difficulty maintaining a consistent meditation routine.

   - *Strategy:*

   - *Set Realistic Goals:* Start with realistic goals, such as a few minutes a day, and gradually increase the duration as you become more comfortable.

   - *Create a Routine:* Integrate meditation into your daily routine, associating it with a specific time or activity. Consistency builds the habit over time.

9. **Feeling Overwhelmed:**

   - *Challenge:* Some individuals may feel overwhelmed by emotions or sensations during meditation.

   - *Strategy:*

   - *Guided Meditations:* Use guided meditations or apps that provide structure and support, especially for emotional exploration.

- *Reduce Duration:* If overwhelming emotions arise, consider shortening the duration of your meditation until you feel more comfortable.

10. **Comparison and Judgement:**

- *Challenge:* Comparing your meditation experience to others or judging yourself for perceived shortcomings.

- *Strategy:*

- *Cultivate Self-Compassion:* Approach your meditation practice with self-compassion. Accept that each meditation session is unique, and progress varies for everyone.

- *Mindful Reflection:* Instead of judgement, reflect mindfully on your experiences without attaching labels of success or failure.

Final Thoughts

Overcoming challenges in meditation is a gradual process that involves patience, self-compassion, and a commitment to the practice. Remember that each meditation session is an opportunity to learn and grow, and challenges are natural aspects of the journey.

Adjust your approach based on what works best for you, and don't hesitate to explore different meditation techniques until you find the ones that resonate with your needs and preferences.

Provide Strategies and Tips for Overcoming These Challenges and Sustaining a Consistent Practice.

Overcoming challenges and sustaining a consistent meditation practice involves a combination of strategies tailored to individual needs. Here are tips to address common challenges and maintain a regular meditation routine:

1. **Start Small:**

   - *Tip:* Begin with short sessions, even just a few minutes a day. Gradually increase the duration as your comfort and familiarity with meditation grow.

2. **Set Realistic Expectations:**

   - *Tip:* Avoid setting overly ambitious goals. Recognise that meditation is a skill that develops over time. Be patient and embrace the learning process.

3. **Establish a Routine:**

   – *Tip:* Integrate meditation into your daily routine. Designate a specific time each day, whether it's morning, lunchtime, or before bed. Consistency is key to forming a habit.

4. **Create a Dedicated Space:**

   – *Tip:* Designate a quiet and comfortable space for meditation. Personalise it to make it inviting and conducive to your practice. Having a dedicated space helps signal the beginning of your meditation session.

5. **Use Guided Meditations:**

   – *Tip:* Utilise guided meditations or meditation apps, especially if you're new to the practice. Guided sessions provide structure and support, guiding you through the process.

6. **Explore Different Techniques:**

   – *Tip:* Experiment with various meditation techniques to find what resonates with you. This could include mindfulness, loving-kindness, body scan, or breath-focused meditation.

7. **Join a Meditation Group:**

   – *Tip:* Consider joining a local or online meditation group. Group settings provide accountability, encouragement, and a sense of community, fostering motivation.

8. **Practice Mindful Walking:**

   – *Tip:* If sitting meditation proves challenging, incorporate mindful walking into your routine. Focus on each step and your breath as you walk, bringing mindfulness into motion.

9. **Use Reminders:**

   – *Tip:* Set reminders on your phone or place visual cues in your environment to prompt your meditation practice. Consistent reminders help reinforce the habit.

10. **Practice Mindful Moments:**

    – *Tip:* Incorporate mindfulness into daily activities, such as eating, commuting, or doing household chores. This cultivates mindfulness throughout the day, making it an integral part of your lifestyle.

11. **Mindful Breathing Breaks:**

    – *Tip:* Take short, mindful breathing breaks throughout the day. Pause for a few moments, focus on your breath, and bring your awareness to the present-moment.

12. **Cultivate Self-Compassion:**

    – *Tip:* Approach your meditation practice with self-compassion. Be kind to yourself, and avoid self-criticism. Understand that challenges are a natural part of the process.

13. **Journaling:**

    – *Tip:* Keep a meditation journal to track your experiences, challenges, and insights. Reflecting on your journey can provide valuable insights and motivation.

14. **Mindful Eating:**

    – *Tip:* Practice mindfulness during meals. Pay attention to the tastes, textures, and sensations of each bite. This can serve as a mindful ritual and a way to integrate mindfulness into daily life.

15. **Celebrate Small Wins:**

   – *Tip:* Acknowledge and celebrate small milestones in your meditation practice. Whether it's a week of consistent practice or a moment of deep presence, recognising these achievements builds positive reinforcement.

16. **Stay Open-Minded:**

   – *Tip:* Be open to adjusting your approach. If a particular technique or time of day doesn't work, explore alternatives. Flexibility and adaptability are essential for sustaining a long-term practice.

17. **Connect with a Teacher:**

   – *Tip:* Consider seeking guidance from a meditation teacher or attending meditation workshops. Having a mentor can offer personalised insights and support for overcoming challenges.

18. **Mindfulness Apps:**

   – *Tip:* Use mindfulness apps that offer guided meditations, progress tracking, and reminders. These apps often provide a structured approach and make meditation accessible.

19. **Engage in Regular Reflection:**

    – *Tip:* Regularly reflect on the positive impact of meditation on your life. Recognise the changes in your mental and emotional well-being as motivation to continue your practice.

20. **Adapt to Changing Circumstances:**

    – *Tip:* Be adaptable in your practice. Life circumstances may change, affecting your routine. Instead of seeing disruptions as setbacks, find ways to adapt your practice to the evolving demands of your life.

Remember that sustaining a consistent meditation practice is a journey that involves self-discovery and adaptation. Be gentle with yourself, stay committed to the process, and celebrate the transformative power that regular meditation can have on your overall well-being.

Spiritual Dimensions of Meditation

Connecting with the Divine: Exploring Different Spiritual Traditions

Connecting with the divine is a fundamental aspect of various spiritual traditions, each offering unique practices and perspectives on how individuals can experience and cultivate this connection. Here's an exploration of connecting with the divine in different spiritual traditions:

1. **Hinduism:**

   – *Deities and Rituals:* Hinduism encompasses a diverse array of deities, and individuals connect with the divine through rituals, prayers (puja), and devotional practices (bhakti yoga).

   – *Meditation and Yoga:* Practices like meditation and yoga are integral to Hindu spirituality, providing pathways to connect with the divine within oneself and the cosmos.

2. **Buddhism:**

   – *Inner Enlightenment:* Buddhism focuses on attaining inner enlightenment and Nirvana. Meditation, particularly mindfulness and concentration practices, is central to this process.

   – *Compassion and Loving-Kindness:* Connecting with the divine is often expressed through cultivating compassion and loving-kindness toward oneself and all sentient beings.

3. **Christianity:**

   – *Prayer and Worship:* Christianity emphasises connecting with God through prayer, worship services, and sacraments. Communion, baptism, and the Eucharist are sacred rituals fostering this connection.

   – *Contemplative Prayer:* Some Christian traditions, such as contemplative Christianity, emphasise silent contemplative prayer to deepen the personal relationship with the divine.

4. **Islam:**

   - *Submission and Surrender:* Islam teaches submission to the will of Allah. Connecting with the divine involves performing the five pillars of Islam, daily prayers (Salah), and engaging in acts of charity and pilgrimage (Hajj).

   - *Sufi Mysticism:* Sufism, the mystical dimension of Islam, employs practices like Dhikr (remembrance of God) and Sufi whirling to induce states of spiritual ecstasy and union with the divine.

5. **Judaism:**

   - *Prayer and Rituals:* Connecting with the divine in Judaism involves prayer, especially through rituals like the Shema. Observing Sabbath, festivals, and engaging in acts of loving-kindness contribute to this connection.

   - *Kabbalah Mysticism:* Kabbalistic teachings delve into the mystical aspects of Judaism, offering practices like meditation on the divine names and visualisation to attain a deeper connection.

6. **Sikhism:**

   – *Simran and Seva:* Sikhs connect with the divine through Simran (remembrance of God) and Seva (selfless service). The Guru Granth Sahib, the holy scripture, is central to this connection.

   – *Langar:* The Sikh practice of Langar, communal meals, reflects the principle of equality and interconnectedness, fostering a sense of divine presence in all.

7. **Taoism:**

   – *Harmony with the Tao:* Taoism teaches aligning with the Tao (the Way) to connect with the divine. Practices like Qigong, Tai Chi, and meditation facilitate this harmonious alignment.

   – *Nature Connection:* Taoist sages often find spiritual connection in nature, viewing the natural world as an expression of the divine order.

8. **Bahá'í Faith:**

   - *Oneness of God and Humanity:* The Bahá'í Faith emphasises the oneness of God, humanity, and religion. Connecting with the divine involves prayer, meditation, and adherence to the teachings of Bahá'u'lláh.

   - *Unity and Equality:* The Bahá'í Faith promotes unity, equality, and the elimination of prejudices, fostering a connection with the divine through the recognition of the divine in every soul.

9. **Native Spiritual Traditions:**

   - *Sacred Rituals and Ceremonies:* Indigenous spiritual traditions often involve connecting with the divine through sacred rituals, ceremonies, and a deep reverence for the land and its spirits.

   - *Ancestral Connection:* Connection with the divine may be intertwined with the honouring of ancestors and seeking guidance from the spiritual forces present in nature.

10. New Age and Spirituality:

- *Personal Growth and Transformation:* New Age spirituality often focuses on personal growth and transformation, using practices like meditation, visualisation, and energy healing to connect with higher consciousness.

- *Exploration of Higher Realms:* New Age practitioners explore various spiritual realms, including angels, spirit guides, and ascended masters, as part of their divine connection.

Common Threads Across Traditions

- *Prayer and Devotion:* Many traditions emphasise the power of prayer and devotional practices as a means of establishing a direct connection with the divine.

- *Meditation and Contemplation:* Across diverse traditions, meditation and contemplative practices serve as pathways to deepen one's connection with the divine, whether through stillness, mindfulness, or visualisation.

- *Love and Compassion:* The expression of love and compassion, both towards oneself and others, is often considered a universal means of connecting with the divine presence.

In conclusion, the ways in which individuals connect with the divine are rich, diverse, and deeply rooted in the cultural, historical, and philosophical contexts of their respective traditions. These practices not only provide a framework for spiritual connection but also foster a sense of purpose, meaning, and transcendence in the lives of those who seek a deeper connection with the divine.

Finding Common Threads and Universal Truths

Despite the rich diversity of spiritual and religious traditions, there are common threads and universal truths that often weave through the tapestry of human beliefs. These shared elements reflect fundamental aspects of the human experience and our collective search for meaning and connection. Here are some common threads and universal truths found across various traditions:

1. **Ethical Principles:**

   - *Commonality:* Virtues such as compassion, kindness, honesty, and justice are emphasised in nearly all traditions.

   - *Universal Truth:* The recognition of ethical values as guiding principles for human conduct is a shared understanding that transcends cultural and religious boundaries.

2. **Golden Rule:**

   - *Commonality:* The idea of treating others as you would like to be treated is present in various forms across traditions.

   - *Universal Truth:* The Golden Rule underscores the importance of empathy, reciprocity, and interconnectedness among individuals and communities.

3. **Connection with the Divine:**

   - *Commonality:* Almost every tradition provides a means for individuals to connect with the divine, whether through prayer, meditation, rituals, or contemplation.

- *Universal Truth:* The human quest for a deeper connection with a higher power or universal source is a pervasive and fundamental aspect of spirituality.

4. **Love and Compassion:**
   - *Commonality:* The importance of love and compassion is a recurring theme in spiritual teachings.
   - *Universal Truth:* Love is often seen as a unifying force that transcends differences and fosters a sense of unity and understanding.

5. **Inner Transformation:**
   - *Commonality:* Many traditions emphasise the inner journey and the transformation of the self.
   - *Universal Truth:* The recognition that personal growth, self-awareness, and inner harmony contribute to a more fulfilling and purposeful life is a shared understanding.

6. **Sacredness of Life:**
   - *Commonality:* Virtually all traditions hold life as sacred and emphasise its inherent value.

- *Universal Truth:* The recognition of the sanctity of life promotes reverence for all living beings and encourages responsible stewardship of the environment.

7. **Impermanence and Change:**

   - *Commonality:* The understanding that everything is subject to change and impermanence is a theme in Eastern philosophies and Western mystical traditions.

   - *Universal Truth:* Acceptance of impermanence fosters resilience, adaptability, and a deeper appreciation for the present-moment.

8. **Unity and Interconnectedness:**

   - *Commonality:* Many traditions acknowledge the interconnectedness of all existence.

   - *Universal Truth:* The recognition of a shared humanity and a sense of oneness with the cosmos promotes harmony, peace, and a collective responsibility for the well-being of the world.

9. **Service to Others:**

- *Commonality:* Acts of service, charity, and selfless giving are virtues across traditions.

- *Universal Truth:* Engaging in service to others is seen as a way to express compassion, contribute to the common good, and transcend self-centredness.

10. **Seeking Wisdom and Truth:**

- *Commonality:* The pursuit of wisdom, truth, and understanding is a common thread in philosophy and spiritual teachings.

- *Universal Truth:* The human quest for knowledge and a deeper understanding of existence is a fundamental aspect of the human experience.

11. **Rituals and Ceremonies:**

- *Commonality:* Rituals and ceremonies, whether communal or personal, are integral to many traditions.

- *Universal Truth:* Rituals provide a structured means for expressing devotion, marking significant life events, and fostering a sense of belonging.

12. **Hope and Faith:**

   - *Commonality:* The presence of hope and faith, often rooted in a belief in a higher power or cosmic order, is a recurring theme.

   - *Universal Truth:* Hope and faith provide solace, resilience, and a sense of purpose in the face of life's challenges

13. **Mindfulness and Presence:**

   - *Commonality:* The practice of mindfulness, being present in the moment, and cultivating awareness are found in various traditions.

   - *Universal Truths:* The recognition of the transformative power of mindfulness in fostering a deeper connection with oneself and the world.

14. **Symbolism and Sacred Spaces:**

   - *Commonality:* The use of symbols, sacred spaces, and rituals to evoke the transcendent is prevalent in religious and spiritual practices.

- *Universal Truth:* Symbolism and sacred spaces serve as conduits for connecting with the divine and expressing reverence.

15. Striving for Inner Peace:

- *Commonality:* The pursuit of inner peace and tranquillity is a common goal across traditions.
- *Universal Truth:* Inner peace is seen as essential for overall well-being, resilience, and the ability to navigate life's challenges.

These common threads and universal truths reflect shared aspects of the human experience that transcend cultural, geographical, and temporal boundaries. They emphasise the interconnectedness of humanity in its collective search for meaning, purpose, and a deeper understanding of the mysteries of existence.

The Power of Gratitude: Cultivating a Spirit of Thankfulness

The power of gratitude is transformative, offering individuals a profound way to cultivate a spirit of thankfulness that can positively impact their mental, emotional, and physical well-being. Gratitude is more than a polite expression; it is a practice that can shape perspectives and enhance the quality of life. Here's an exploration of the power of gratitude:

1. **Shift in Perspective:**

   – *Cognitive Rewiring:* Gratitude encourages a shift from a mindset of scarcity to abundance, allowing individuals to focus on what they have rather than what they lack.

   – *Positive Reframing:* By reframing challenges as opportunities for growth, gratitude enables individuals to find meaning even in difficult circumstances.

2. **Emotional Well-Being:**

   – *Positive Emotions:* Regular expressions of gratitude are linked to increased levels of positive emotions such as joy, love, and contentment.

   – *Stress Reduction:* Gratitude has been shown to reduce stress and enhance emotional resilience, helping individuals cope with life's inevitable ups and downs.

3. **Enhanced Relationships:**

   – *Connection:* Expressing gratitude strengthens social bonds, fostering a sense of connection and mutual support.

   – *Reciprocity:* Gratitude often leads to a positive feedback loop, as individuals who feel appreciated are more likely to reciprocate with kindness.

4. **Physical Health Benefits:**

   – *Stress Reduction:* Gratitude is associated with lower levels of cortisol, the stress hormone, contributing to overall physical well-being.

- *Improved Sleep:* Practicing gratitude has been linked to better sleep quality and duration.

5. **Resilience in Adversity:**

   - *Adaptive Coping:* Gratitude acts as a buffer during challenging times, fostering adaptive coping strategies and a sense of hope.

   - *Perspective Amidst Challenges:* It helps individuals find silver linings and lessons in adversity, promoting resilience.

6. **Mindfulness and Presence:**

   - *Present-Moment Awareness:* Gratitude encourages mindfulness by anchoring individuals in the present-moment, fostering an appreciation for life as it unfolds.

   - *Savouring Experiences:* It prompts individuals to savour positive experiences, deepening their engagement with life.

7. **Self-Reflection and Personal Growth:**

   - *Introspection:* Gratitude invites self-reflection, encouraging individuals to recognise personal strengths, values, and areas for growth.

- *Continuous Development:* It promotes a growth mindset by acknowledging progress and the potential for ongoing personal development.

8. **Generosity and Altruism:**

   - *Generous Behaviour:* Grateful individuals are more likely to engage in prosocial behaviours, contributing to the well-being of others.

   - *Altruistic Motivation:* Gratitude fosters a desire to give back, creating a positive impact on communities and fostering a sense of interconnectedness.

9. **Optimism and Positivity:**

   - *Positive Outlook:* Gratitude is associated with increased optimism, helping individuals approach life with a more positive and hopeful mindset.

   - *Appreciation for Simple Joys:* It encourages individuals to find joy in everyday experiences, fostering a sense of wonder and appreciation.

10. Spiritual Connection:

- *Transcendence:* Gratitude is often intertwined with spiritual practices, providing a pathway to connect with something greater than oneself.

- *Humility:* Recognising and appreciating the gifts of life instils a sense of humility, acknowledging the mysteries and interconnectedness of existence.

11. Cultivation of Contentment:

- *Satisfaction with What Is:* Gratitude promotes contentment by highlighting the value of the present-moment and the positive aspects of one's life.

- *Reduced Materialism:* Grateful individuals are often less driven by materialistic pursuits, finding fulfilment in non-material aspects of life.

12. Expressing Gratitude:

- *Verbal and Written Acknowledgement:* Expressing gratitude through words, writing in a gratitude journal, or even simple acts of kindness conveys appreciation.

- *Reinforcing Positive Behaviour:* Acknowledging and reinforcing positive behaviour in oneself and others creates a culture of gratitude.

13. Community Building:

- *Collective Well-Being:* Cultivating gratitude on a societal level contributes to a collective sense of well-being, promoting harmony and cooperation.

- *Gratitude Practices in Groups:* Shared expressions of gratitude in families, workplaces, or communities strengthen social bonds and foster a positive atmosphere.

14. Daily Practice and Rituals:

- *Gratitude Journaling:* Keeping a gratitude journal, where individuals regularly note things they are thankful for, reinforces the habit of recognising blessings.

- *Morning or Evening Reflection:* Taking a few moments each day to reflect on gratitude contributes to a positive and mindful start or end to the day.

15. Universal Principle:

- *Cross-Cultural Significance:* Gratitude is a universal principle found in diverse cultures and religions, emphasising its inherent value in the human experience.

- *Timeless Wisdom:* The timeless wisdom of gratitude is echoed in ancient philosophies, religious texts, and contemporary positive psychology.

Cultivating a spirit of thankfulness through the practice of gratitude is a transformative journey that touches various facets of life. Whether through individual reflections, acts of kindness, or communal expressions, gratitude has the power to enhance well-being, foster positive relationships, and contribute to a more harmonious and resilient society.

Discussing the Role of Gratitude in Spiritual Development

Gratitude plays a significant and transformative role in spiritual development, serving as a key practice across various religious and philosophical traditions. Its influence extends beyond mere appreciation; it becomes a profound way for individuals to connect with the divine, foster spiritual growth, and deepen their understanding of the sacred. Here's a discussion on the role of gratitude in spiritual development:

1. **Acknowledging Divine Gifts:**

   – *Recognition of Blessings:* Gratitude is a fundamental aspect of acknowledging and appreciating the gifts bestowed by the divine, whether it's the gift of life, health, relationships, or opportunities.

   – *Deepening Connection:* Expressing gratitude for these divine gifts fosters a sense of connection with the sacred, recognising the benevolence inherent in the fabric of existence.

2. **Cultivating Humility:**

   – *Acknowledging Higher Power:* Gratitude cultivates humility by acknowledging a higher power or universal force that contributes to the richness of life.

   – *Understanding Interconnectedness:* Recognising the interconnectedness of all things encourages a humble acknowledgement of one's place in the vast tapestry of creation.

3. **Prayer and Devotion:**

   - *Gratitude as Prayer:* In many spiritual traditions, gratitude is expressed through prayers and devotional practices, where individuals thank the divine for guidance, protection, and blessings.

   - *Deepening Devotion:* Regular expressions of gratitude deepen the sense of devotion and strengthen the spiritual bond between the individual and the divine.

4. **Transformative Power:**

   - *Shift in Consciousness:* Gratitude brings about a shift in consciousness, moving individuals from a self-centred perspective to an awareness of the divine presence in every aspect of life.

   - *Transcending Ego:* The practice of gratitude facilitates the transcendence of ego-driven desires and fosters a focus on the divine will.

5. **Opening the Heart:**

   - *Generosity and Love:* Gratitude opens the heart to generosity and love, allowing individuals to share their blessings with others and embody the divine qualities of compassion and kindness.

- *Receptivity to Grace:* A grateful heart becomes receptive to divine grace, allowing individuals to experience a profound sense of spiritual abundance.

6. **Facing Challenges with Grace:**

   - *Resilience in Adversity:* Gratitude serves as a source of strength and resilience during challenging times, helping individuals find meaning and lessons in the face of adversity.

   - *Trusting the Divine Plan:* Grateful individuals often trust in the wisdom of the divine plan, accepting that challenges are part of a larger, purposeful journey.

7. **Mindful Presence:**

   - *Present-Moment Awareness:* Gratitude encourages individuals to be present in the moment, fostering a mindful awareness of the divine presence in everyday experiences.

   - *Savouring the Divine in Each Moment:* Spiritual development is enriched by the practice of savouring the divine essence within the ordinary and extraordinary moments of life.

8. **Promoting Self-Reflection:**

   - *Inner Inquiry:* Gratitude prompts self-reflection, inviting individuals to explore their values, beliefs, and the ways in which they align with the divine principles.

   - *Spiritual Inventory:* Regularly expressing gratitude involves taking stock of one's spiritual journey, acknowledging growth, and recognising areas for further development.

9. **Acts of Worship and Service:**

   - *Gratitude as Worship:* Gratitude is often intertwined with acts of worship, as individuals express thanks through rituals, ceremonies, and acts of devotion.

   - *Service as Devotion:* Grateful hearts are naturally inclined towards selfless service, viewing acts of kindness and service to others as expressions of love and devotion to the divine.

10. Fostering a Positive Spiritual Atmosphere:

- *Community and Collective Gratitude:* In spiritual communities, collective expressions of gratitude create a positive and uplifting atmosphere, fostering a shared sense of divine presence.

- *Energising Spiritual Practices:* Gratitude infuses energy into spiritual practices, making rituals and gatherings more meaningful and potent.

11. Building a Foundation for Faith:

- *Faith in Divine Providence:* Gratitude nurtures faith by instilling confidence in the divine providence that guides and sustains individuals on their spiritual journey.

- *Trusting the Unseen:* Grateful individuals often learn to trust in the unseen, cultivating a deeper faith that goes beyond mere belief.

12. Alignment with Spiritual Values:

- *Living in Accordance with Principles:* Gratitude aligns individuals with spiritual values such as love, compassion, forgiveness, and humility.

- *Integrating Virtues:* Regular practice of gratitude contributes to the integration of virtues into daily life, fostering spiritual maturation.

13. **Celebration of Sacred Moments:**

- *Gratitude as Celebration:* Spiritual development involves celebrating sacred moments and expressing gratitude for the divine presence in milestones, rites of passage, and moments of spiritual insight.

- *Marking Spiritual Growth:* Grateful acknowledgement of personal and collective growth becomes a form of spiritual celebration and acknowledgement of the divine unfolding.

14. **Facilitating Surrender:**

- *Letting Go and Trusting:* Gratitude facilitates surrender by encouraging individuals to let go of attachments, fears, and desires, trusting in the divine order of life.

- *Surrender as Spiritual Liberation:* Surrendering with gratitude becomes a pathway to spiritual liberation, allowing individuals to experience a profound sense of freedom and peace.

15. Integration into Spiritual Practices:

- *Gratitude Rituals:* Many spiritual traditions incorporate gratitude rituals, such as offering thanks before meals, expressing gratitude during prayer, or incorporating gratitude into meditation practices.
- *Integration into Spiritual Disciplines:* Gratitude becomes an integral part of spiritual disciplines, enhancing the efficacy of practices and contributing to a holistic approach to spiritual development.

In summary, gratitude is a dynamic and transformative force in spiritual development. Its multifaceted influence encompasses humility, devotion, resilience, mindfulness, and the nurturing of virtues. The practice of gratitude is not just an external expression; it becomes an internal state of being that shapes the way individuals perceive and interact with the divine, fostering a profound journey of spiritual growth and connection.

Offering Practical Exercises for Cultivating Gratitude

Cultivating gratitude is a transformative practice that can be integrated into daily life through various exercises. These exercises are designed to help individuals develop a habit of recognising and appreciating the positive aspects of their lives. Here are some practical exercises for cultivating gratitude:

1. **Gratitude Journaling:**

   - *Exercise:* Set aside a few minutes each day to write down three things you are grateful for. These can be simple or profound, ranging from the smell of fresh coffee to moments of personal growth.

   - *Benefits:* Regularly journaling gratitude helps focus attention on positive experiences, fostering a more optimistic outlook.

2. **Three Good Things:**

   - *Exercise:* At the end of each day, reflect on three positive things that happened. Consider why they occurred and express gratitude for those moments.

- *Benefits:* This exercise promotes a positive mindset by encouraging individuals to consciously seek and appreciate positive aspects of their day.

3. **Gratitude Letter:**

   - *Exercise:* Write a letter expressing gratitude to someone who has had a positive impact on your life. Be specific about the actions or qualities you appreciate.

   - *Benefits:* Not only does this exercise cultivate gratitude, but sharing the letter can deepen connections and bring joy to both the writer and the recipient.

4. **Gratitude Jar:**

   - *Exercise:* Place an empty jar in a visible place. Whenever you experience something for which you are grateful, write it on a small piece of paper and place it in the jar.

   - *Benefits:* The jar becomes a visual reminder of the abundance of positive experiences, fostering a sense of gratitude over time.

5. **Mindful Appreciation:**

   – *Exercise:* Engage in a mindful appreciation exercise by fully savouring a specific moment or experience. Use your senses to immerse yourself in the details.

   – *Benefits:* Mindful appreciation deepens the experience of gratitude by bringing awareness to the richness of the present-moment.

6. **Morning Gratitude Ritual:**

   – *Exercise:* Start your day by reflecting on three things you are grateful for. This can be done during meditation, prayer, or simply while sipping your morning beverage.

   – *Benefits:* Setting a positive tone in the morning influences the outlook for the rest of the day.

7. **Gratitude Walk:**

   – *Exercise:* Take a mindful walk, focusing on the beauty of your surroundings. Express gratitude for the colours, sounds, and sensations you experience.

- *Benefits:* Connecting with nature and expressing gratitude during a walk promotes a sense of well-being.

8. **Gratitude Meditation:**

   - *Exercise:* Practice gratitude meditation by sitting in a comfortable position, focusing on your breathing, and gradually bringing to mind things for which you are grateful.

   - *Benefits:* Regular meditation deepens the neural pathways associated with gratitude, making it a more ingrained and natural response.

9. **Gratitude Affirmations:**

   - *Exercise:* Create daily affirmations that express gratitude. Repeat these affirmations throughout the day, either silently or aloud.

   - *Benefits:* Affirmations reinforce positive thinking patterns and shift the focus toward gratitude.

10. **Family or Group Gratitude Sharing:**

    - *Exercise:* During family dinners or group gatherings, take turns sharing something you are grateful for. Encourage everyone to participate.

- *Benefits:* Group expressions of gratitude foster a positive and connected atmosphere.

11. Random Acts of Kindness:

- *Exercise:* Perform small acts of kindness for others without expecting anything in return. Reflect on the positive impact of your actions.

- *Benefits:* Acts of kindness generate a sense of gratitude both in the giver and the recipient.

12. Gratitude Vision Board:

- *Exercise:* Create a vision board that visually represents things you are grateful for or aspire to have in your life.

- *Benefits:* A vision board serves as a visual reminder of your blessings and aspirations, reinforcing a mindset of gratitude.

13. Gratitude for Challenges:

- *Exercise:* Reflect on challenging situations and identify lessons or positive aspects that have emerged. Express gratitude for the growth opportunities.

- *Benefits:* Recognising the silver lining in challenges fosters resilience and a deeper understanding of life's complexities.

14. Digital Detox Gratitude:

- *Exercise:* Designate a specific time each week for a digital detox. Use this time to appreciate the offline world, nature, or personal connections.

- *Benefits:* Disconnecting from digital devices allows for a more mindful and gratitude-focused experience.

15. Seasonal Gratitude Rituals:

- *Exercise:* Create rituals around seasons or holidays that involve expressing gratitude. This could include a gratitude circle during Thanksgiving or a nature appreciation activity during spring.

- *Benefits:* Incorporating gratitude into seasonal rituals adds depth and meaning to the celebrations.

Tips

- *Consistency:* Establish a regular practice to make gratitude a habit.
- *Specificity:* Be specific when expressing gratitude, focusing on details rather than generalities.
- *Reflective Pause:* Take a moment to reflect on why you are grateful for a particular experience or person.
- *Variety:* Experiment with different exercises to find what resonates best with you.

Cultivating gratitude is an ongoing journey that, over time, enhances well-being, fosters positive relationships, and contributes to a more fulfilling and purposeful life.

Inner Healing: Addressing Emotional and Spiritual Wounds

Inner healing is a profound and transformative process that addresses emotional and spiritual wounds, fostering recovery, growth, and a renewed sense of well-being. It involves a holistic approach to understanding, acknowledging, and ultimately transforming the deep-seated pain or trauma that individuals may carry. Here's a discussion on inner healing, encompassing its principles, methods, and the integration of emotional and spiritual well-being:

1. **Understanding Inner Healing:**

   – *Holistic Perspective:* Inner healing recognises the interconnectedness of the emotional, mental, and spiritual aspects of an individual.

   – *Transformational Journey:* It involves a journey of self-discovery, self-compassion, and the intentional pursuit of healing and wholeness.

2. **Principles of Inner Healing:**

   – *Compassionate Self-Awareness:* Inner healing begins with a compassionate awareness of one's emotions, thoughts, and spiritual state.

   – *Acceptance and Forgiveness:* Embracing acceptance of oneself and others, coupled with the practice of forgiveness, are foundational principles.

   – *Connection with the Divine:* Many approaches to inner healing involve cultivating a connection with a higher power, divine source, or spiritual principles.

3. **Acknowledging Emotional Wounds:**

   – *Exploration of Pain:* Inner healing requires an honest exploration of past and present emotional wounds, trauma, or unmet needs.

   – *Validation:* Acknowledging and validating one's emotional pain is a crucial step towards healing.

4. **Spiritual Dimensions of Inner Healing:**

   – *Faith and Trust:* For many, inner healing involves placing faith and trust in a higher power or spiritual principles.

   – *Transcendence:* It often includes a transcendent experience where individuals connect with a sense of purpose, meaning, or divine guidance.

5. **Healing Modalities:**

   – *Therapeutic Approaches:* Inner healing can be facilitated through various therapeutic modalities such as psychotherapy, counselling, or holistic healing practices.

   – *Mindfulness and Meditation:* Practices that promote mindfulness and meditation are often incorporated to bring awareness to the present-moment and facilitate healing.

6. **Emotional Release Techniques:**

   – *Artistic Expression:* Engaging in artistic expression, such as writing, painting, or music, can serve as a powerful outlet for emotional release.

- *Body-Centred Therapies:* Techniques like somatic experiencing or yoga aim to release emotional tension stored in the body.

7. **Guided Visualisation and Inner Work:**

   - *Inner Child Work:* Exploring and nurturing the inner child is a common aspect of inner healing, addressing unresolved issues from childhood.

   - *Guided Visualisation:* Visualisation techniques are employed to create positive and healing inner experiences.

8. **Mind-Body Connection:**

   - *Holistic Approach:* Recognising the intricate connection between the mind and body, inner healing often involves practices that promote physical well-being alongside emotional and spiritual healing.

   - *BreathworkandEnergyHealing:* Techniques like breathwork and energy healing address the energetic and physiological aspects of healing.

9. **Community and Support Systems:**

   - *Social Connection:* Building supportive relationships and participating in a community that encourages healing and growth is integral.

   - *Group Therapy:* Group settings provide a safe space for individuals to share experiences, gain insights, and receive support.

10. **Integration of Faith and Beliefs:**

    - *Spiritual Guidance:* Seeking guidance from spiritual leaders, mentors, or engaging in practices aligned with one's faith can be a source of strength.

    - *Prayer and Rituals:* Incorporating prayer, rituals, or spiritual ceremonies into the healing process is common.

11. **Holistic Self-Care:**

    - *Nutrition and Exercise:* Inner healing involves holistic self-care practices that encompass physical health, emphasising nutrition and exercise.

- *Rest and Relaxation:* Adequate rest and relaxation contribute to emotional and spiritual well-being.

12. **Mindfulness and Presence:**
    - *Present-Moment Awareness:* Mindfulness practices cultivate an awareness of the present-moment, allowing individuals to observe and release emotional pain.
    - *Mindful Living:* Integrating mindfulness into daily life fosters a more conscious and intentional way of being.

13. **Reframing and Positive Psychology:**
    - *Cognitive Restructuring:* Inner healing often involves reframing negative thought patterns and adopting a more positive and empowering perspective.
    - *Strength-Based Approaches:* Positive psychology principles emphasise identifying and leveraging personal strengths for healing and growth.

14. **Transformation and Growth:**
    - *Alchemy of Pain*: Inner healing views pain and challenges as opportunities for transformation and growth.

- *Emergence of Authentic Self:* The process facilitates the emergence of one's authentic self, liberated from the constraints of past wounds.

15 Continual Self-Reflection:

- *Lifelong Journey:* Inner healing is recognised as an ongoing, lifelong journey of self-reflection, self-compassion, and personal evolution.

- *Embracing Change:* Individuals learn to embrace change, viewing it as a natural and necessary part of the journey towards wholeness.

In summary, inner healing is a dynamic and multifaceted process that addresses emotional and spiritual wounds through a holistic and integrative approach. By combining self-awareness, spiritual connection, therapeutic modalities, and supportive practices, individuals embark on a transformative journey towards healing, self-discovery, and a renewed sense of purpose and well-being.

Exploring the Intersection of Spirituality and Emotional Well-being

The intersection of spirituality and emotional well-being is a profound and intricate realm where the dimensions of the inner self and the transcendent converge. This intersection involves recognising the impact of spiritual beliefs, practices, and experiences on emotional health. Here's an exploration of how spirituality and emotional well-being intersect:

1. **Meaning and Purpose:**

   – *Spiritual Framework:* Spirituality often provides a framework for understanding the deeper meaning and purpose of life.

   – *Emotional Well-Being:* Having a sense of purpose and meaning contributes to emotional well-being, offering a foundation for resilience in the face of challenges.

2. **Connection and Belonging:**

   – *Spiritual Community:* Participation in a spiritual community fosters a sense of connection and belonging.

   – *Emotional Support:* Belonging to a supportive community can provide emotional support during times of joy or difficulty.

3. **Mindfulness and Presence:**

   – *Spiritual Practices:* Many spiritual practices, such as meditation and prayer, emphasise mindfulness and present-moment awareness.

   – *Emotional Regulation:* Mindfulness enhances emotional regulation by promoting self-awareness and the ability to respond to emotions in a measured way.

4. **Compassion and Forgiveness:**

   – *Spiritual Principles:* Compassion and forgiveness are often emphasised in spiritual teachings.

   – *Emotional Healing:* Practicing compassion and forgiveness contributes to emotional healing, reducing resentment and promoting a positive emotional state.

5. **Transcendence and Perspective:**

   – *Spiritual Transcendence:* Experiences of transcendence in spirituality can shift perspectives and offer a broader view of life.

- *Emotional Resilience:* Transcendent experiences often contribute to emotional resilience, helping individuals navigate challenges with greater ease.

6. **Rituals and Ceremonies:**

   - *Spiritual Rituals:* Rituals and ceremonies in spiritual practices provide a structured way to express and process emotions.

   - *Emotional Expression:* Engaging in meaningful rituals can serve as a healthy outlet for emotional expression and release.

7. **Hope and Coping:**

   - *Spiritual Hope:* Spiritual beliefs often provide a source of hope, especially in difficult circumstances.

   - *Emotional Coping:* Hope is a crucial factor in emotional coping, helping individuals persevere through adversity.

8. **Self-Reflection and Growth:**

   - Spiritual Inquiry: Spiritual practices often encourage self-reflection and a quest for personal growth.

- *Emotional Insight:* Self-reflection contributes to emotional intelligence, fostering a deeper understanding of one's emotions and promoting growth.

9. **Gratitude and Contentment:**

   - *Spiritual Gratitude:* Many spiritual traditions emphasise the practice of gratitude.

   - *Emotional Contentment:* Cultivating gratitude contributes to emotional contentment and a positive outlook on life.

10. **Values and Emotional Alignment:**

    - *Spiritual Values:* Spirituality often involves the identification of core values and principles.

    - *Emotional Alignment:* Living in alignment with one's values enhances emotional well-being, fostering a sense of authenticity and fulfilment.

11. **Empathy and Connection:**

    - *Spiritual Empathy:* Spiritual practices often cultivate empathy and compassion for others.

- *Emotional Connection:* Developing empathy strengthens emotional connections with others, promoting a sense of shared humanity.

12. Faith and Trust:

- *Spiritual Faith:* Faith in a higher power or universal order is a central aspect of many spiritual beliefs.

- *Emotional Trust:* Faith contributes to emotional trust, providing a sense of security and reassurance during uncertain times.

13. Sacred Spaces and Tranquillity:

- *Spiritual Spaces:* Places of worship or natural settings are often considered sacred in spiritual traditions.

- *Emotional Tranquillity:* Spending time in sacred spaces can evoke a sense of tranquillity and emotional peace.

14. Altruism and Emotional Fulfilment:

- *Spiritual Altruism:* Spiritual teachings often emphasise the importance of selfless acts and service to others.

- *Emotional Fulfilment:* Engaging in acts of altruism contributes to emotional fulfilment and a sense of purpose.

15. Integration and Wholeness:

- *Holistic Approach:* Spirituality encourages a holistic understanding of the self, encompassing emotional, mental, and spiritual dimensions.

- *Emotional Wholeness:* Embracing a holistic perspective fosters emotional wholeness, recognising the interconnected nature of the human experience.

In summary, the intersection of spirituality and emotional well-being is a dynamic and reciprocal relationship. Spiritual beliefs and practices influence emotional health, providing a framework for understanding, coping, and thriving in the face of life's challenges. Conversely, emotional well-being enhances the depth and authenticity of spiritual experiences, creating a synergistic and enriching interplay between the inner self and the transcendent. The exploration of this intersection offers individuals a pathway to cultivate resilience, meaning, and emotional flourishing in their personal journey.

Tips for Incorporating Tools into Daily Life

- *Consistency:* Make these practices a regular part of your routine.
- *Gentleness:* Approach yourself with gentleness and patience; healing is a gradual process.
- *Adaptability:* Explore different tools and find what resonates most with you.
- *Integration:* Integrate tools into your daily life, weaving them seamlessly into your activities.

Remember, the journey of inner healing and self-compassion is unique to each individual. Be kind to yourself as you explore these tools, and embrace the process of growth and transformation.

Discussing the Challenges of Balancing Spirituality With a Busy Life

Balancing spirituality with a busy life can indeed be challenging, as the demands of a hectic schedule often leave little time for contemplation and reflection. However, recognising these challenges and finding effective solutions is crucial for maintaining a sense of inner peace and alignment with spiritual principles. Here are some common challenges and strategies to navigate them:

1. **Time Constraints:**

   – *Challenge:* Busy schedules often leave little time for spiritual practices.

   – *Solution:* Prioritise spiritual activities by scheduling them into your day. Even brief moments of mindfulness or prayer can make a significant impact.

2. **Distractions and Multitasking:**

   – *Challenge:* Constant distractions and multitasking can hinder deep spiritual engagement.

   – *Solution:* Create dedicated spaces for spiritual practices, limit screen time, and focus on one task at a time to enhance mindfulness.

3. **Overwhelm and Stress:**

   – *Challenge:* Busy lives can lead to stress and overwhelm, making it challenging to stay connected spiritually.

- *Solution:* Incorporate stress-reducing practices like meditation, deep breathing, or yoga. Recognise the importance of taking breaks to maintain balance.

4. **External Expectations:**
   - *Challenge:* External expectations from work or society may conflict with personal spiritual values.
   - *Solution:* Clearly define your values and communicate boundaries. Make conscious choices that align with your spiritual principles.

5. **Guilt for 'Non-Productive' Time:**
   - *Challenge:* Guilt may arise when taking time for spiritual practices, which is perceived as unproductive.
   - *Solution:* Recognise the value of spiritual well-being. Understand that investing time in your spiritual growth contributes to overall life satisfaction.

6. **Lack of Community Support:**
   - *Challenge:* Lack of understanding or support from your immediate community can be isolating.

- *Solution:* Seek like-minded individuals or communities both online and offline. Share your experiences and challenges, and build a supportive network.

7. **Struggle to Maintain Consistency:**

   - *Challenge:* Inconsistent routines make it difficult to maintain spiritual practices.

   - *Solution:* Start with small, manageable steps. Set realistic goals and gradually build up consistency over time.

8. **Feeling Disconnected:**

   - *Challenge:* A busy life may lead to a sense of disconnection from your spiritual self.

   - *Solution:* Integrate spiritual practices into daily activities. Find moments for reflection during routine tasks or commutes.

9. **Comparison with Others:**

   - *Challenge:* Comparing your spiritual journey with others can lead to feelings of inadequacy.

- *Solution:* Embrace your unique path. Focus on your personal growth rather than external benchmarks.

10. **Inability to Attend Spiritual Gatherings:**

    - *Challenge:* Busy schedules may hinder attendance at spiritual gatherings or community events.

    - *Solution:* Explore virtual options, such as online classes or forums. Participate in local events when possible, and create your own sacred space at home.

11. **Balancing Material and Spiritual Goals:**

    - *Challenge:* Striking a balance between material pursuits and spiritual aspirations can be challenging.

    - *Solution:* Align your material goals with your spiritual values. Seek fulfilment in both realms without compromising one for the other.

12. **Lack of Personal Reflection Time:**

    - *Challenge:* Constant busyness may leave little time for personal reflection and introspection.

– *Solution:* Designate specific times for reflection. Disconnect from external stimuli and create a peaceful space for self-awareness.

13. Integration of Spirituality at Work:

– *Challenge:* Integrating spiritual principles into a demanding work environment may seem impractical.

– *Solution:* Identify ways to infuse spirituality into your work, such as maintaining ethical practices, finding purpose in your work, and taking short breaks for mindful moments.

14. Mindless Consumption of Information:

– *Challenge:* Busyness can lead to mindless consumption of information, leaving little room for intentional learning or spiritual growth.

– *Solution:* Set boundaries on information consumption. Choose quality over quantity and engage in purposeful learning.

15. Fear of Missing Out (FOMO):

- *Challenge:* Fear of missing out on social or professional opportunities can create internal conflict.

- *Solution:* Evaluate opportunities based on your spiritual values. Prioritise those that align with your authentic self rather than succumbing to external pressures.

Tips for Overcoming Challenges

- *Start Small:* Begin with manageable spiritual practices that can be easily incorporated into your routine.

- *Flexibility:* Be flexible with your spiritual routine. Adapt practices based on the demands of each day.

- *Mindful Scheduling:* Intentionally schedule time for spiritual activities, treating them with the same priority as other commitments.

- *Set Boundaries:* Clearly define boundaries for work, social commitments, and personal time.

- *Delegate Responsibilities:* Delegate tasks when possible, reducing the burden of responsibilities.

- *Consistent Reminders:* Use reminders or alarms to prompt moments of mindfulness or reflection throughout the day.

Balancing spirituality with a busy life requires intentional effort and a commitment to nurturing your inner self amid external demands. By acknowledging these challenges and implementing practical strategies, you can cultivate a harmonious integration of spirituality into your daily existence. Remember that the journey is unique for each individual, and finding a rhythm that resonates with your lifestyle is a continuous process of adaptation and self-discovery.

Love and Compassion: The Heart of Spiritual Living

Love and compassion are often considered the heart of spiritual living, transcending religious and philosophical boundaries. These qualities form the essence of a meaningful and fulfilling spiritual journey, contributing to personal growth, interpersonal relationships, and a deep connection with the larger universe. Here's an exploration of love and compassion as the core of spiritual living:

1. **Unconditional Love:**

   - *Essence:* Spiritual living emphasises the practice of unconditional love—a love that is not bound by conditions or expectations.

   - *Impact:* Unconditional love fosters acceptance, understanding, and a sense of interconnectedness with all living beings.

2. **Compassion Towards Self and Others:**

   – *Self-Compassion:* Spiritual living encourages individuals to extend compassion towards themselves, acknowledging imperfections and fostering self-love.

   – *Interpersonal Compassion:* Compassion towards others involves understanding their suffering and actively working towards alleviating it.

3. **Forgiveness:**

   – *Foundational Principle:* Forgiveness is a core aspect of love and compassion in spiritual teachings.

   – *Transformation:* Forgiving oneself and others is seen as a transformative process that liberates the heart from resentment and fosters healing.

4. **Kindness as a Practice:**

   – *Daily Practice:* Kindness is not just an act but a way of life in spiritual traditions.

- *Ripple Effect:* Acts of kindness create a ripple effect, positively influencing individuals and communities.

5. **Empathy and Understanding:**

   - *Connection:* Spiritual living encourages the development of empathy, the ability to understand and share the feelings of others.

   - *Harmony:* Cultivating empathy promotes harmonious relationships and bridges the gaps between different perspectives.

6. **Service to Others:**

   - *Selfless Giving:* Service to others, without expecting anything in return, is a fundamental expression of love and compassion.

   - *Spiritual Growth:* Engaging in acts of service contributes to personal spiritual growth and a sense of purpose.

7. **Connection with the Divine:**

   - *Devotion:* Love towards a higher power or the divine is a common theme in spiritual living.

- *Surrender:* Surrendering to this love fosters a sense of trust, peace, and alignment with a greater purpose.

8. **Generosity and Sharing:**

   - *Abundance Mentality:* Spiritual living encourages an abundance mentality, where individuals share generously without fear of scarcity.

   - *Collective Well-Being:* Generosity contributes to the well-being of the collective, emphasising the interconnectedness of all beings.

9. **Gratitude as a Spiritual Practice:**

   - *Attitude of Gratitude:* Gratitude is viewed as an essential spiritual practice.

   - *Shift in Perspective:* Cultivating gratitude transforms one's perspective, emphasising appreciation for life's blessings.

10. **Heart-Centred Living:**

    - *Living from the Heart:* Spiritual living encourages individuals to live from the heart rather than solely from the mind.

- *Emotional Intelligence:* This approach promotes emotional intelligence, empathy, and a deeper understanding of oneself and others.

11. Mindful Relationships:

- *Present in Relationships:* Spiritual teachings emphasise being fully present in relationships.

- *Harmony and Connection:* Mindful relationships lead to harmony, deeper connections, and the mutual growth of individuals.

12. Non-Judgemental Attitude:

- *Release of Judgement:* Love and compassion entail releasing judgement towards oneself and others.

- *Freedom:* A non-judgemental attitude allows for freedom and acceptance of diverse experiences and paths.

13. Cultivation of Inner Peace:

- *Inner Harmony:* Love and compassion contribute to inner peace, irrespective of external circumstances.

- *Radiating Peace:* Individuals who embody love and compassion become agents of peace, influencing their surroundings positively.

14. Unity Consciousness:

- *Oneness with All:* Spiritual living often emphasises the concept of unity consciousness.
- *Global Perspective:* Recognising the interconnectedness of all life fosters a global perspective that transcends individual, societal, or cultural boundaries.

15. Transformation Through Love:

- *Power to Transform:* Love is seen as a transformative force that can heal wounds, inspire change, and elevate consciousness.
- *Personal and Collective Evolution:* The power of love is considered instrumental in personal and collective evolution.

Practices to Cultivate Love and Compassion

- *Loving-Kindness Meditation:* A practice that involves sending love and goodwill to oneself and others.

- *Random Acts of Kindness:* Engage in small, unexpected acts of kindness throughout the day.

- *Heart-Centred Prayer:* Include prayers focused on love, compassion, and the well-being of others.

- *Daily Affirmations:* Affirmations that emphasise love, forgiveness, and compassion can reshape thought patterns.

- *Empathetic Listening:* Listen attentively and empathetically to others, seeking to understand their perspectives.

In essence, love and compassion serve as the guiding principles of spiritual living, shaping attitudes, actions, and relationships. Embracing these qualities not only contributes to personal well-being but also fosters a more harmonious and compassionate world. The journey of spiritual living involves a continual deepening of these qualities, leading to profound inner transformation and a positive impact on the broader human experience.

Exploring the Transformative Power of Love and Compassion

The transformative power of love and compassion is profound, touching every aspect of human existence and fostering personal growth, interpersonal harmony, and societal well-being. Here's an exploration of how love and compassion wield their transformative influence:

1. **Self-Transformation:**

   – *Self-Love and Acceptance:* Love and compassion towards oneself initiate a journey of self-discovery and acceptance.

   – *Healing Past Wounds:* Compassion facilitates healing by allowing individuals to forgive themselves and release emotional burdens.

2. **Empathy and Understanding:**

   – *Connecting Across Differences:* Compassion enables individuals to understand and connect with others, transcending cultural, social, and personal differences.

- *Promoting Unity:* Love and empathy foster a sense of unity, breaking down barriers that often lead to division and conflict.

3. **Healing Relationships:**

   - *Forgiveness:* Love and compassion are integral to the forgiveness process, mending relationships and fostering reconciliation.

   - *Creating Trust:* Acts of compassion build trust, strengthening the foundation of meaningful connections.

4. **Promoting Altruism:**

   - *Selfless Giving:* Compassion inspires acts of altruism, promoting a culture of selfless service to others.

   - *Global Impact:* Altruistic actions contribute to positive global change, addressing societal challenges with empathy and kindness.

5. **Cultivating Resilience:**

   - *Emotional Resilience:* Love and compassion cultivate emotional resilience, helping individuals navigate challenges with grace and strength.

- *Positive Outlook:* A compassionate perspective encourages a positive outlook, even in the face of adversity.

6. **Encouraging Gratitude:**

   - *Appreciation for Life:* Love fosters a deep appreciation for life's experiences, leading to a more grateful and contented existence.

   - *Countering Negativity:* Compassion counters negativity, redirecting focus towards the positive aspects of life.

7. **Creating a Culture of Kindness:**

   - *Ripple Effect:* Acts of love and kindness create a ripple effect, influencing individuals and communities.

   - *Social Harmony:* A culture of kindness promotes social harmony, enhancing the overall well-being of society.

8. **Emotional Intelligence:**

   - *Understanding Emotions:* Love and compassion enhance emotional intelligence, allowing individuals to understand and manage their own emotions and the emotions of others.

- *Empathy in Leadership:* Compassionate leaders demonstrate a higher level of emotional intelligence, fostering supportive and inclusive work environments.

9. **Fostering Inner Peace:**

   - *Transcending Conflict:* Love and compassion help individuals transcend inner conflicts, leading to a sense of inner peace.

   - *Embracing Stillness:* Compassion cultivates a calm and centred mind, allowing for moments of introspection and clarity.

10. **Inspiring Personal Growth:**

    - *Encouraging Exploration:* Love encourages individuals to explore their potential and pursue personal growth.

    - *Facing Challenges:* Compassion provides the strength needed to face challenges, transforming difficulties into opportunities for learning and development.

11. **Environmental Stewardship:**

    - *Love for Nature:* Compassion extends to the environment, promoting responsible and sustainable practices.

- *Global Consciousness:* A love for the planet encourages collective efforts towards environmental conservation and protection.

12. Cultivating Mindfulness:

- *Present-Moment Awareness:* Love and compassion anchor individuals in the present-moment, fostering mindfulness.

- *Reducing Stress:* Mindful living, rooted in love, contributes to stress reduction and overall well-being.

13. Encouraging Interconnectedness:

- *Spiritual Connection:* Compassion nurtures a sense of interconnectedness, acknowledging the spiritual bond that unites all living beings.

- *Global Unity:* Recognising our interconnectedness promotes a global perspective, encouraging collaboration for the greater good.

14. Transformation of Societal Norms:

- *Challenging Prejudices:* Love challenges societal norms that perpetuate prejudices, discrimination, and inequality.

- *Advocacy for Justice:* Compassion inspires advocacy for social justice, contributing to the transformation of oppressive systems.

15. Spiritual Awakening:

- *Deepening Spiritual Connection:* Love and compassion are integral to spiritual awakening, deepening one's connection with the divine or universal consciousness.

- *Transcending Ego:* Compassion helps individuals transcend the ego, leading to a more profound understanding of the self and others.

Practices to Harness the Transformative Power

- *Loving-Kindness Meditation:* A meditation practice focused on cultivating love and compassion towards oneself and others.

- *Random Acts of Kindness:* Engage in spontaneous acts of kindness to spread love and positivity.

- *Compassionate Listening:* Listen with empathy, seeking to understand the emotions and perspectives of others.

– Forgiveness Rituals: Develop rituals or practices to aid in the process of forgiving oneself and others.

– *Mindful Presence:* Be fully present at the moment, practicing mindfulness in daily activities.

The transformative power of love and compassion is an ongoing journey—one that begins within the individual and radiates outward to influence relationships, communities, and the world at large. As these qualities become ingrained in daily life, they create a ripple effect, contributing to a more compassionate, understanding, and harmonious global society.

Discussing Ways to Cultivate a Compassionate Heart

Cultivating a compassionate heart is a transformative journey that involves intentional practices and a shift in mindset. Here are ways to foster and nurture a compassionate heart:

1. **Self-Reflection:**

   – *Inner Inquiry:* Reflect on your own experiences, emotions, and responses.

- *Understanding Suffering:* Recognise your own suffering and use it as a bridge to understand the pain of others.

2. **Cultivate Empathy:**

   - *Put Yourself in Others' Shoes:* Practice seeing situations from different perspectives.

   - *Active Listening:* Listen with the intent to understand, not just to respond.

3. **Practice Loving-Kindness Meditation:**

   - *Metta Meditation:* Engage in loving-kindness meditation, extending well-wishes and compassion to yourself and others.

   - *Regular Practice:* Make it a consistent part of your meditation routine to strengthen feelings of compassion.

4. **Learn from Compassionate Role Models:**

   - *Identify Inspirations:* Identify individuals who embody compassion and learn from their actions.

   - *Study Biographies:* Read about the lives of compassionate figures to gain insights and inspiration.

5. **Cultivate Mindfulness:**

   - *Present-Moment Awareness:* Be fully present in your interactions and activities.

   - *Observe Without Judgement:* Mindfulness allows you to observe situations without immediate judgement, fostering compassion.

6. **Practice Compassionate Communication:**

   - *Choose Words Wisely:* Be mindful of the words you use, ensuring they convey understanding and kindness.

   - *Express Empathy:* Respond to others with empathy, acknowledging their feelings and experiences.

7. **Engage in Acts of Kindness:**

   - *Small Acts Matter:* Perform random acts of kindness regularly.

   - *Service to Others:* Engage in volunteer work or activities that benefit others without expecting anything in return.

8. **Forgiveness Practices:**

   - *Release Resentment:* Practice forgiveness towards yourself and others.

   - *Letting Go:* Understand that forgiveness is for your own peace and not necessarily for the benefit of the other person.

9. **Cultivate a Gratitude Practice:**

   - *Daily Reflection:* Reflect on the things you're grateful for each day.

   - *Appreciate Abundance:* Cultivate a sense of abundance, reducing the tendency to focus on lack.

10. **Connect with Nature:**

    - *Nature Walks:* Spend time in nature to connect with the beauty and interconnectedness of the natural world.

    - *Environmental Awareness:* Foster a compassionate heart by recognising the importance of environmental stewardship.

11. **Educate Yourself:**

    - *Understand Diverse Perspectives:* Educate yourself about different cultures, religions, and perspectives.

- *Awareness of Social Issues:* Stay informed about social issues to cultivate compassion for those facing adversity.

12. Engage in Self-Care:

- *Mind-Body Connection:* Recognise the connection between your mental and physical well-being.
- *Nurture Yourself:* Ensure adequate self-care to be more available for others.

13. Mindful Consumption of Media:

- *Conscious Media Choices:* Be mindful of the media you consume, choosing content that promotes understanding and empathy.
- *Limit Negative Inputs:* Reduce exposure to content that fuels negativity and divisiveness.

14. Join Compassionate Communities:

- *Supportive Networks:* Surround yourself with communities that share and promote compassionate values.
- *Collective Action:* Engage in collective efforts to contribute to positive change in your community.

15. **Celebrate Diversity:**

- *Embrace Differences:* Cultivate an appreciation for the richness of diversity in all its forms.

- *Open-Mindedness:* Challenge your own biases and prejudices, fostering a more inclusive perspective.

16. **Mindful Breathing and Loving-Kindness Breathwork:**

- *Conscious Breathing:* Practice mindful breathing to centre yourself and cultivate a calm, open heart.

- *Loving-Kindness Breathwork:* Combine breathwork with loving-kindness intentions for a deeper sense of compassion.

17. **Engage in Compassionate Visualisation:**

- *Imaginative Compassion:* Visualise situations where compassion is needed and imagine responding with empathy and kindness.

- *Creating Positive Scenarios:* This practice helps create a mental blueprint for compassionate behaviour.

18. **Read Compassionate Literature:**

 - *Inspiring Stories:* Read literature that tells stories of compassion, resilience, and acts of kindness.

 - *Philosophical Texts:* Explore philosophical works that delve into the nature of compassion and love.

19. **Attend Compassion Workshops or Retreats:**

 - *Guided Learning:* Participate in workshops or retreats focused on cultivating compassion.

 - *Interactive Exercises:* Engage in interactive exercises to deepen your understanding and practice.

20. **Regularly Reevaluate Intentions:**

 - *Mindful Intentions:* Regularly reassess your intentions in various situations.

 - *Course Correction:* Make adjustments to align your actions with compassionate intentions.

Cultivating a compassionate heart is an ongoing practice that requires patience and self-reflection.

By incorporating these strategies into your daily life, you can gradually transform your mindset and actions, fostering a genuine and deep sense of compassion for yourself and the world around you.

The Journey Continues: Sustaining and Sharing Spiritual Growth

The journey of spiritual growth is a continuous, evolving process that extends beyond personal development to include sustaining one's progress and sharing the wisdom gained with others. Here are key aspects of the journey that go beyond individual growth:

1. **Sustaining Personal Spiritual Growth:**

   - *Continual Practice:* Sustaining spiritual growth involves regular and consistent spiritual practices such as meditation, prayer, or mindfulness.

   - *Lifelong Learning:* Cultivate a mindset of continuous learning, exploring new spiritual teachings and insights.

2. **Integration into Daily Life:**

   – *Seamless Integration:* Spiritual growth is most impactful when integrated seamlessly into daily life.

   – *Mindful Living:* Practice mindfulness and awareness in all activities, fostering a deep connection with the present-moment.

3. **Embracing Challenges as Opportunities:**

   – *Resilience:* View challenges as opportunities for spiritual growth rather than obstacles.

   – *Mindset Shift:* Adopt a growth-oriented mindset, recognising that challenges contribute to personal and spiritual development.

4. **Cultivating Virtues and Ethical Living:**

   – *Living Ethical Principles:* Sustain spiritual growth by aligning actions with ethical and moral principles.

   – *Cultivating Virtues:* Focus on cultivating virtues such as compassion, kindness, and gratitude in daily interactions.

5. **Connection with a Spiritual Community:**

   – *Community Support:* Engage with a spiritual community for mutual support and shared growth.

   – *Collective Practices:* Participate in group meditation, prayer circles, or other communal practices to reinforce spiritual connections.

6. **Service to Others:**

   – *Selfless Giving:* Extend spiritual growth by engaging in acts of service and selfless giving.

   – *Compassionate Action:* Look for opportunities to contribute to the well-being of others and the broader community.

7. **Deepening the Inner Journey:**

   – *Inner Exploration:* Continue exploring the depths of the inner self through introspection and self-discovery.

   – *Advanced Practices:* Consider advanced spiritual practices or deepen existing ones to further the inner journey.

8. **Maintaining a Beginner's Mind:**

   – *Curiosity and Openness:* Sustain growth by maintaining a beginner's mind—approaching life with curiosity, openness, and a willingness to learn.

   – *Avoiding Complacency:* Resist the temptation to become complacent in your spiritual journey; embrace the evolving nature of personal growth.

9. **Creative Expression and Artistic Pursuits:**

   – *Spiritual Artistry:* Explore creative expression as a form of spiritual practice.

   – *Connecting with the Divine Through Art:* Engage in artistic pursuits that facilitate a connection with the divine or higher consciousness.

10. **Cultivating Gratitude:**

    – *Daily Reflection:* Sustain spiritual growth by incorporating daily gratitude practices.

    – *Gratitude Journaling:* Keep a journal to document moments of gratitude and reflection on the spiritual journey.

11. Mentoring and Guiding Others:

- *Sharing Wisdom:* Mentor others on their spiritual journey by sharing your insights and experiences.
- *Guiding with Compassion:* Offer guidance with empathy and compassion, recognising that each individual's path is unique.

12. Mindful Communication:

- *Conscious Expression:* Practice mindful communication, ensuring that your words align with your spiritual values.
- *Deep Listening:* Foster meaningful connections through deep listening and empathetic communication.

13. Ecological and Environmental Awareness:

- *Stewardship of Nature:* Extend spiritual growth to include a heightened awareness of environmental issues.
- *Sustainable Living:* Adopt sustainable practices that reflect a sense of responsibility for the well-being of the planet.

14 Celebrating Milestones:

- *Reflective Moments:* Pause to celebrate and reflect on personal spiritual milestones.

- *Gratitude for Growth:* Express gratitude for the progress made and the insights gained on the spiritual journey.

15. Adapting to Change:

- *Flexibility:* Sustain spiritual growth by remaining flexible and adaptable in the face of life's changes.

- *Resilience in Transition:* Use spiritual principles to navigate transitions and challenges with resilience.

16. Global and Universal Connection:

- *Universal Love:* Expand spiritual growth by cultivating a sense of universal love for all beings.

- *Global Awareness:* Develop an awareness of global issues and contribute to positive change on a larger scale.

17. **Sustaining Humility:**

- *Humility in Growth:* Remain humble in the face of spiritual growth, acknowledging that the journey is ongoing.

- *Learning from Others:* Embrace the opportunity to learn from others, regardless of their spiritual background or experience.

18. **Integration of Wisdom Traditions:**

- *Interfaith Understanding:* Deepen spiritual growth by exploring wisdom traditions beyond one's own.

- *Integration of Insights:* Integrate insights from diverse traditions to enrich your spiritual perspective.

19. **Art of Letting Go:**

- *Detachment:* Cultivate the art of letting go, releasing attachments to outcomes and embracing the flow of life.

- *Inner Freedom:* Find inner freedom by surrendering to the present-moment and accepting the impermanence of life.

20. Evolving the Concept of Self:

- *Transcending Ego:* Sustain spiritual growth by transcending the limitations of the ego.
- *Connecting with the Higher Self:* Foster a deeper connection with the higher self, acknowledging the interconnected nature of all existence.

Sustaining and sharing spiritual growth involves a holistic approach that encompasses personal practices, community engagement, ethical living, and a commitment to continual learning. By embracing the journey with an open heart and a willingness to contribute to the well-being of others, individuals can create a ripple effect of positive transformation in themselves and the world around them.

Discussing the Ongoing Nature of the Spiritual Journey

The spiritual journey is an ongoing, dynamic process characterised by continuous growth, self-discovery, and evolving understanding. Unlike a destination, it is a path that unfolds over time, presenting opportunities for transformation, challenges, and deepening insights. Here are key aspects highlighting the ongoing nature of the spiritual journey:

1. **Continuous Self-Discovery:**

   – The spiritual journey involves an ever-deepening exploration of the self. As individuals evolve, new layers of consciousness and aspects of their identity come to light.

   – Continuous self-discovery means confronting and understanding both the light and shadow aspects of one's personality.

2. **Dynamic Nature of Beliefs:**

   – Beliefs and perspectives are not fixed but evolve over time. As individuals grow spiritually, their understanding of fundamental truths may expand, shift, or become more nuanced.

   – The journey invites individuals to question and refine their beliefs, fostering a more inclusive and expansive worldview.

3. **Adapting to Change:**

   – Life is marked by constant change, and the spiritual journey requires adaptability. As circumstances evolve, individuals must navigate transitions, challenges, and new opportunities.

- Adapting to change involves applying spiritual principles to maintain inner balance and resilience.

4. **Integration of Lessons:**

   - Lessons learned on the spiritual journey are not isolated events but contribute to a cumulative process of growth. Experiences are integrated into the fabric of one's being.

   - Reflecting on and learning from past experiences is essential for ongoing development.

5. **Lifelong Learning:**

   - The spiritual journey is an educational odyssey, emphasising the importance of lifelong learning. Whether through formal study, personal experiences, or insights gained in daily life, there is always room to expand one's knowledge and wisdom.

   - A curious and open mind fosters continual growth.

6. **Cyclical Nature of Challenges:**

   - Challenges are inherent to the spiritual journey, and they often recur in different forms. Each challenge provides an opportunity for deeper understanding, resilience, and spiritual maturation.

   - Facing challenges with equanimity contributes to ongoing inner strength.

7. **Evolution of Practices:**

   - Spiritual practices are not static but evolve to meet the changing needs of the individual. As one progresses, meditation, prayer, or mindfulness techniques may deepen or take on new forms.

   - Exploring diverse practices contributes to a richer spiritual experience.

8. **Interconnectedness with Others:**

   - Relationships play a vital role in the spiritual journey, serving as mirrors that reflect aspects of the self. Interactions with others provide opportunities for growth, compassion, and understanding.

- The ongoing journey involves cultivating harmonious and meaningful connections.

9. **Deepening Connection with the Divine:**

   - Spiritual growth involves an ever-deepening connection with the divine or higher consciousness. This connection may evolve from intellectual understanding to a profound, experiential communion.

   - Practices such as prayer, meditation, or contemplation contribute to deepening this connection.

10. **Embracing Paradoxes:**

    - The spiritual journey often involves navigating paradoxes and embracing the coexistence of opposites. This may include finding peace within chaos or discovering unity within diversity.

    - Accepting paradoxes allows for a more holistic and inclusive spiritual perspective.

11. **Integration of Mind, Body, and Spirit:**

    - The holistic nature of the spiritual journey emphasises the integration of mind, body, and spirit. The ongoing process involves maintaining balance in these aspects of one's being.

- Practices such as yoga, mindful movement, or energy work contribute to this integration.

12. A Journey Beyond Goals:

- Unlike achievement-oriented pursuits, the spiritual journey is not goal-driven in the conventional sense. It is more about the unfolding process than reaching a specific destination.

- Embracing the journey itself, rather than fixating on outcomes, fosters a sense of presence and fulfilment.

13. Transcending Dualities:

- Spiritual growth often entails transcending dualities, such as good and bad, success and failure, or pleasure and pain. This involves moving beyond judgement and cultivating equanimity.

- The ongoing journey invites individuals to navigate life's contrasts with greater grace.

14. The Role of Presence:

- Presence is a cornerstone of the spiritual journey. Being fully present in each moment allows for a deeper connection with the self, others, and the divine.

- Cultivating mindfulness and presence contributes to a more profound and enriching spiritual experience.

15. Incorporating Spirituality into Daily Life:

- The spiritual journey is not confined to specific moments of practice but extends into daily life. It involves embodying spiritual principles in actions, relationships, and decision-making.

- Infusing daily life with mindfulness and conscious living is a testament to the ongoing nature of the journey.

16. Understanding the Illusory Nature of Ego:

- As individuals progress on the spiritual journey, there is an evolving awareness of the illusory nature of the ego. Recognising and transcending the ego's limitations is an ongoing process.

- Letting go of ego-driven attachments contributes to a more liberated and authentic existence.

17. Embracing Mystery and Uncertainty:

- The spiritual journey acknowledges the inherent mystery and uncertainty of life. Embracing the unknown becomes a way of navigating the unfolding path.

- Trusting in the mystery fosters a sense of surrender and openness to the infinite possibilities of the spiritual journey.

18. Cultivating Heart-Centred Living:

- The ongoing journey often leads individuals to shift from a solely intellectual understanding to a heart-centred way of living. Compassion, love, and empathy become guiding principles.

- Cultivating a heart-centred approach contributes to a more meaningful and interconnected existence.

19. Spiritual Evolution Beyond Traditions:

- The spiritual journey transcends religious or cultural boundaries. Individuals may find resonance with multiple traditions or forge a unique path that aligns with their personal growth.

- Exploring diverse spiritual perspectives contributes to a more inclusive understanding of the journey.

20. Legacy of Wisdom:

- The ongoing spiritual journey leaves a legacy of wisdom. Sharing insights, teachings, and experiences with others becomes a natural outgrowth of the evolving path.
- Contributing to the collective wisdom of humanity becomes a way of giving back and fostering the spiritual growth of future generations.

In essence, the spiritual journey is an ever-unfolding process, where the true essence lies in the journey itself rather than reaching a destination. Embracing the ongoing nature of this journey involves openness, adaptability, and a commitment to continual growth and self-discovery. It is a dynamic pilgrimage that leads individuals towards a deeper understanding of themselves, their connection to others, and the profound mysteries of existence.

Encouraging Readers to Share Their Spiritual Insights and Practices With Others

Encouraging others to share their spiritual insights and practices can create a supportive and enriching community where individuals can learn from each other's experiences. Here's a message to inspire readers to share their spiritual journey with others:

- Dear Seekers of Spiritual Wisdom,

Embarking on a spiritual journey is a deeply personal endeavour, a quest for meaning, connection, and higher understanding. Yet, as we traverse our individual paths, we discover that the beauty of spirituality is not solely found in solitary moments but in the shared tapestry of collective wisdom.

Your insights, experiences, and practices are unique, like a precious gem contributing to the mosaic of our shared human experience. As you navigate the landscapes of your soul, consider the transformative power of extending a hand to others on similar journeys.

Why Share Your Spiritual Insights?

1. **Mutual Inspiration:** Your journey may inspire someone who is facing similar challenges or seeking answers to profound questions.

2. **Collective Growth:** By sharing, you contribute to a collective pool of wisdom that benefits the entire community.
3. **Connection:** In the sharing of vulnerabilities and triumphs, we build bridges of understanding, fostering a sense of shared humanity.

How to Share

1. **Write from the Heart:** Whether it's a personal anecdote, a revelation, or a timeless lesson, let your words reflect the authenticity of your spiritual journey.
2. **Create a Safe Space:** Encourage open dialogue and a non-judgemental atmosphere where others feel comfortable sharing their experiences.
3. **Celebrate Diversity:** Recognise that spiritual paths are diverse. Embrace different perspectives, beliefs, and practices, cultivating an inclusive environment.
4. **Share Practices:** If you have discovered transformative practices, rituals, or meditations, consider sharing them. Your tools might become a guiding light for someone else.

Your Invitation

- *Share Your Light:* Imagine the impact of your words resonating with a fellow seeker, offering guidance, solace, or a new perspective. Your unique voice matters.
- *Create Community:* In sharing, we form connections that transcend the limitations of physical boundaries. Your story might be the encouragement someone needs to embark on their own journey.
- *Elevate Together:* Let's rise together. Your contribution, no matter how small, contributes to the collective elevation of consciousness.

Remember, your journey is a beacon that can illuminate the paths of others. Share your light, your wisdom, and your heart. Together, let's weave a tapestry of spiritual growth and mutual understanding.

With love and shared light,

[Your Name]

Share your insights below and let the journey of collective wisdom begin!

Managing Spiritual Life and Material Life

Balancing spiritual life and material life is a common challenge faced by many individuals in the modern world. The pursuit of spiritual growth and enlightenment doesn't necessarily conflict with living a material life; it's about finding harmony and integration. Here are some suggestions to help you manage both aspects effectively:

1. **Set Clear Priorities:**
   - Clearly define your priorities and values. Understand what is truly important to you in both your spiritual and material pursuits. This clarity can guide your decision-making process.
2. **Mindful Time Management:**
   - Allocate time intentionally for both spiritual practices and material responsibilities. Create a schedule that allows you to engage in spiritual activities, such as meditation or prayer, while also fulfilling your work, family, and social commitments.
3. **Integrate Spirituality into Daily Life:**
   - Bring spiritual principles into your daily activities. Practice mindfulness,

compassion, and gratitude in your interactions with others and in your work. This integration helps bridge the gap between spiritual and material aspects of life.

4. **Align Work with Purpose:**

   – Seek work that aligns with your values and sense of purpose. When your profession is in harmony with your spiritual principles, it becomes a means of expressing and deepening your spiritual values.

5. **Practice Non-Attachment:**

   – Cultivate a sense of non-attachment to material possessions and outcomes. Recognise that material success is impermanent and does not define your true essence. This perspective can help you navigate challenges with equanimity.

6. **Simplify and Declutter:**

   – Simplify your life by decluttering both physically and mentally. Let go of unnecessary possessions, thoughts, and commitments that do not contribute to your well-being or spiritual growth.

7. **Financial Mindfulness:**

   – Manage your finances mindfully. Consider your spending habits and align them with your values. Avoid excessive materialism and strive for financial stability without succumbing to the pressure of constant consumerism.

8. **Connect with Like-Minded Individuals:**

   – Build a supportive community of individuals who share similar spiritual values. This can provide encouragement, understanding, and shared experiences as you navigate the challenges of balancing spiritual and material aspects of life.

9. **Self-Care Practices:**

   – Prioritise self-care to maintain physical, mental, and emotional well-being. Regular exercise, proper nutrition, and adequate rest contribute to a healthy balance between the material and spiritual dimensions of life.

10. **Regular Retreats and Reflection:**

   – Take periodic breaks for retreats or quiet reflection. This allows you to reassess your priorities, reconnect with your spiritual goals, and gain perspective on the interplay between your spiritual and material life.

11. **Gratitude Practice:**

   - Cultivate a daily gratitude practice. Acknowledge and appreciate the blessings in your life, both material and spiritual. This practice fosters a positive mindset and helps you maintain a balanced perspective.

12. **Adaptability and Flexibility:**

   - Life is dynamic, and circumstances change. Cultivate adaptability and flexibility in your approach to both spiritual and material aspects of life. Be open to learning and adjusting your course as needed.

Remember that achieving balance is a continuous process, and it's okay to recalibrate your priorities and practices as you evolve on your journey. The key is to approach life holistically, integrating spiritual values into your everyday experiences while fulfilling your material responsibilities.

Balancing Spiritual Life and Family

Balancing spiritual life and family life is a common challenge, as both aspects are significant and demand time and attention. Striking a balance between the two requires thoughtful planning, communication, and integration of spiritual practices into daily family life. Here are some practical tips to help you find harmony between your spiritual journey and family responsibilities:

1. **Communication:**

   – Talk openly with your family members about your spiritual practices, values, and the importance of balancing both spiritual and family life. Encourage open communication so that everyone's needs and expectations are understood.

2. **Shared Spiritual Practices:**

   – Integrate spiritual practices that can involve the whole family. This might include family prayer time, meditation sessions, or engaging in volunteer or service activities together. Making spirituality a family affair fosters a sense of unity and shared purpose.

3. **Establish Family Rituals:**

   – Create family rituals or traditions that align with your spiritual values. This could be weekly family dinners, holiday celebrations, or moments of reflection. Rituals help build a sense of connection and provide opportunities for shared spiritual experiences.

4. **Mindful Presence:**

   – Be fully present with your family when you are together. Practice mindfulness and avoid distractions such as electronic devices during family time. Quality time spent with loved ones contributes to a fulfilling family life.

5. **Set Priorities:**

   – Clearly define your priorities and allocate time accordingly. Understand the most important aspects of your spiritual and family life, and make choices that align with those priorities. This may involve setting boundaries on certain activities to ensure dedicated family time.

6. **Flexible Schedule:**

   – Create a flexible schedule that allows for both spiritual practices and family commitments. Be adaptable and willing to adjust your routine based on the needs of your family while ensuring you carve out time for your spiritual pursuits.

7. **Involve Family in Spiritual Learning:**

   – Share your spiritual journey with your family and involve them in your learning process. This could include discussing spiritual books, attending workshops or classes together, or exploring shared interests that align with your spiritual values.

8. **Encourage Individual Spiritual Exploration:**

   – Recognise that family members may have different spiritual needs and interests. Encourage individual spiritual exploration and support each person's unique path, allowing space for personal growth and development.

9. **Delegate and Share Responsibilities:**

   – Distribute household responsibilities among family members to avoid one person feeling overwhelmed. This enables everyone to contribute to the well-being of the family while allowing time for personal and spiritual pursuits.

10. Plan Family Retreats:

– Consider planning occasional family retreats or vacations with a spiritual focus. These can provide dedicated time for relaxation, reflection, and deepening your spiritual connection as a family.

11. Practice Gratitude:

– Cultivate a family culture of gratitude. Express appreciation for each other and for the blessings in your lives. A positive and grateful mindset can enhance the overall well-being of the family.

12. Seek Support:

– Connect with other families who are also balancing spiritual and family life. Share experiences, insights, and challenges with like-minded individuals who can provide support and understanding.

Remember that achieving balance is an ongoing process, and it's normal for priorities and circumstances to evolve over time. By fostering open communication, integrating spiritual practices into family life, and maintaining flexibility, you can create a harmonious balance between your spiritual journey and your family life.

Illusion and Impermanence

'Illusion' and 'impermanence' are fundamental concepts in various philosophical, spiritual, and religious traditions. They provide insights into the nature of existence and the way we perceive and interact with the world.

Illusion

1. **Maya (Hinduism):**

   – In Hindu philosophy, the concept of Maya refers to the illusionary nature of the material world. It suggests that the physical reality we perceive is not the ultimate truth but a veiled, temporary manifestation.

2. **Samsara (Buddhism):**

   – Buddhism teaches about the illusory nature of the world through the concept of Samsara, the cycle of birth, death, and rebirth. The pursuit of enlightenment involves recognising the impermanence and illusory nature of the material world.

3. **Allegory of the Cave (Plato):**

   – In Plato's 'Allegory of the Cave,' he describes individuals who are chained in a cave, perceiving shadows on the wall as reality. The allegory illustrates how our perceptions may be limited or distorted, leading to an understanding of the illusory nature of appearances.

4. **Anicca (Buddhism):**

   – Anicca, or impermanence, is one of the Three Marks of Existence in Buddhism. It highlights the ever-changing nature of all things. Recognising impermanence helps to detach from attachments and cravings that contribute to suffering.

Impermanence

1. **Anitya (Hinduism):**

   – Similar to Buddhism, Hinduism also acknowledges the concept of impermanence through Anitya. This understanding is central to the idea of cosmic cycles, where creation, preservation, and destruction are ongoing processes.

2. **Taoism:**

   – Taoism emphasises the natural flow of life and the impermanence of all things. The Tao Te Ching speaks of the unchanging Tao as the source of all change, emphasising the cyclical nature of existence.

3. **Christianity:**

   – While Christianity may not explicitly use the term impermanence, the idea of the transient nature of life is found in biblical passages such as "For the things we see now will soon be gone, but the things we cannot see will last forever" (2 Corinthians 4:18, NLT).

4. **Modern Philosophy:**

   – Existentialist philosophers like Jean-Paul Sartre and Albert Camus explore the impermanence of life and the inherent lack of meaning. Existentialism often grapples with the human experience of confronting the temporality of existence.

Connection:

- The concepts of illusion and impermanence are interconnected. The illusion refers to the deceptive nature of our perceptions, making us believe in a stable, unchanging reality. Recognising impermanence is a key step in dispelling this illusion, as it involves understanding that all things are in a constant state of flux and change.

- Acceptance of impermanence can lead to a more profound understanding of the illusory nature of attachments and desires. The pursuit of lasting fulfilment through transient phenomena becomes a source of suffering when one recognises the impermanent nature of those phenomena.

In summary, the recognition of illusion and impermanence is a transformative realisation found in various cultural and philosophical traditions. It invites individuals to explore the deeper, more enduring aspects of existence beyond the ephemeral and illusory aspects of the material world.

Spiritual Enlightenment

Enlightenment is a complex and multifaceted concept that has been explored and interpreted in various ways across different philosophical, religious, and cultural traditions. The term is used to describe a state of profound understanding, insight, or awareness that transcends ordinary consciousness. Here are several perspectives on what enlightenment entails:

1. **Buddhism:**

   - In Buddhism, enlightenment, or 'Bodhi,' is the state of perfect wisdom and liberation from the cycle of birth and death (samsara). It is often associated with the attainment of Nirvana, where one experiences the cessation of suffering and the extinguishing of craving and ignorance.

2. **Hinduism:**

   - In Hinduism, enlightenment is often linked to self-realisation and the recognition of one's true nature (Atman). It involves transcending the illusion of individual identity (ego) and realising oneness with the ultimate reality (Brahman). Various paths, such as Jnana Yoga (path of knowledge) and

Bhakti Yoga (path of devotion), can lead to enlightenment.

3. **Western Philosophy:**

   – Enlightenment in Western philosophy is often associated with the Age of Enlightenment (17th and 18th centuries), characterised by an emphasis on reason, science, and individual rights. Philosophers like Immanuel Kant and John Locke explored the idea of intellectual enlightenment and human progress through reason and education.

4. **Taoism:**

   – In Taoism, enlightenment is connected to aligning with the Tao, the natural way of the universe. It involves cultivating a deep understanding of the Tao and living in harmony with the spontaneous flow of life.

5. **Christian Mysticism:**

   – Christian mystics speak of a state of divine illumination or union with God. The goal is to attain a deeper, direct experience of the divine presence and a profound understanding of the mysteries of faith.

6. **Zen Buddhism:**

   – In Zen Buddhism, enlightenment is often referred to as 'Satori' or a sudden, direct experience of the nature of reality. It involves seeing through the illusions of the mind and perceiving the world without conceptual filters.

7. **New Age Spirituality:**

   – In the New Age movement, enlightenment is associated with personal and spiritual growth, expanded consciousness, and a shift in perception. It often involves practices such as meditation, energy healing, and exploration of altered states of consciousness.

8. **Psychology:**

   – In psychological terms, enlightenment might be seen as a state of profound self-awareness and integration. It involves transcending the limitations of the ego, resolving inner conflicts, and achieving a sense of inner peace and balance.

While the interpretations and paths toward enlightenment differ, some common themes include the transcendence of the ego, the realisation of fundamental truths, a deep sense of interconnectedness, and liberation from suffering or ignorance. The concept is rich and nuanced, reflecting the diverse ways in which humanity has sought to understand the nature of existence and the human experience.

Living Without Discriminations

Living without discriminations involves cultivating a mindset and adopting behaviours that embrace diversity, respect differences, and promote inclusivity. Discrimination can manifest in various forms, including those related to race, ethnicity, gender, religion, sexual orientation, disability, and more. Here are some principles and practices that contribute to living without discrimination:

1. **Cultivate Empathy:**

   - Develop the ability to understand and share the feelings of others. Put yourself in others' shoes to gain a deeper understanding of their experiences and perspectives.

2. **Promote Open-Mindedness:**

   - Keep an open mind and be willing to consider alternative viewpoints. Avoid preconceived judgements or stereotypes based on superficial characteristics.

3. **Educate Yourself:**

   – Continuously educate yourself about different cultures, backgrounds, and experiences. Seek out diverse sources of information to broaden your understanding of the world.

4. **Challenge Stereotypes:**

   – Be aware of stereotypes and challenge them when you encounter them. Stereotypes often contribute to discrimination by oversimplifying and distorting the reality of diverse individuals and groups.

5. **Practice Inclusive Language:**

   – Use language that is inclusive and respectful. Avoid derogatory terms or expressions that perpetuate stereotypes or reinforce discriminatory attitudes.

6. **Be Mindful of Unconscious Bias:**

   – Recognise that everyone has unconscious biases. Reflect on your own biases and work towards minimising their impact on your thoughts and actions.

7. **Support Inclusive Policies:**

   – Advocate for and support policies that promote diversity and inclusion. This could include workplace policies, educational initiatives, or community programmes that aim to create equitable opportunities for everyone.

8. **Encourage Diversity in Media Consumption:**

   – Consume a diverse range of media, including books, movies, and news sources, that represent various perspectives. This helps to counteract biases that can be perpetuated by limited exposure to diverse voices.

9. **Engage in Cross-Cultural Experiences:**

   – Actively seek out opportunities to engage with people from different cultural backgrounds. Participate in events, workshops, or activities that facilitate cross-cultural understanding.

10. **Speak Up Against Discrimination:**

   – Be an ally by speaking up against discriminatory behaviour when you witness it. Advocate for those who may be marginalised or facing discrimination.

11. **Encourage Diversity in Leadership:**

   – Support efforts to increase diversity in leadership roles. Encourage organisations to promote inclusivity in decision-making processes.

12. **Foster Inclusive Environments:**

   – Create environments, whether at work, in educational institutions, or in social settings, that are welcoming and respectful of diversity. Foster a sense of belonging for everyone.

13. **Teach and Model Inclusivity:**

   – If you are a parent, educator, or influencer, teach and model inclusive behaviour. Instil values of respect, acceptance, and appreciation for diversity in those you influence.

Living without discrimination requires a conscious effort to challenge biases, promote understanding, and create environments that celebrate the richness of human diversity. It is an ongoing process that involves both individual reflection and collective action.

Leading a Peaceful Life

Leading a peaceful life involves cultivating a mindset and adopting practices that promote inner calm, harmony with others, and a positive impact on the world around you. Here are some principles and practices that can contribute to a more peaceful and fulfilling life:

1. **Cultivate Mindfulness:**

   – Practice mindfulness by staying fully present in the moment. This can be achieved through meditation, deep breathing exercises, or simply paying attention to your surroundings and sensations.

2. **Practice Gratitude:**

   – Foster a sense of gratitude by regularly acknowledging and appreciating the positive aspects of your life. Focus on what you have rather than what you lack.

3. **Develop Inner Peace:**

   – Work on inner peace through self-reflection, forgiveness, and letting go of resentment. Embrace a serene mindset that remains undisturbed by external circumstances.

4. **Foster Positive Relationships:**

   – Surround yourself with positive and supportive relationships. Cultivate empathy, compassion, and effective communication in your interactions with others.

5. **Set Healthy Boundaries:**

   – Establish and maintain healthy boundaries in your personal and professional life. Knowing when to say 'no' and prioritising self-care contributes to overall well-being.

6. **Practice Self-Care:**

   – Take care of your physical, mental, and emotional well-being. Get enough sleep, engage in activities you enjoy, and prioritise self-care practices that recharge your energy.

7. **Simplify Your Life:**

   – Simplify your lifestyle by decluttering your physical space and organising your priorities. Reducing unnecessary complexities can create a sense of calm and focus.

8. **Accept Impermanence:**

   – Embrace the reality of impermanence. Understand that change is a natural part of life, and cultivating flexibility and adaptability can ease the impact of unexpected challenges.

9. **Practice Forgiveness:**

   – Let go of grudges and practice forgiveness. Holding onto resentment and anger only adds to inner turmoil. Forgiveness is a powerful way to release negative emotions and move forward.

10. **Live with Purpose:**

    – Identify and live in alignment with your values and purpose. Knowing your life's purpose provides a sense of direction and fulfilment.

11. **Engage in Relaxation Techniques:**

   - Incorporate relaxation techniques into your routine, such as yoga, tai chi, or nature walks. These activities can help reduce stress and promote a sense of tranquillity.

12. **Limit Exposure to Negative Influences:**

   - Be mindful of the media and influences to which you expose yourself. Limit exposure to negative news or toxic relationships that can disrupt your sense of peace.

13. **Practice Mindful Communication:**

   - Engage in mindful and compassionate communication. Strive to listen actively and express yourself with kindness and clarity.

14. **Contribute to Others:**

   - Engage in acts of kindness and contribute to the well-being of others. Helping others can bring a sense of purpose and satisfaction.

15. **Embrace Nature:**

   - Spend time in nature. Whether it's a walk in the park or a hike in the mountains, connecting with the natural world can bring a sense of peace and perspective.

Leading a peaceful life is a holistic endeavour that involves tending to various aspects of your well-being. It's an ongoing journey that requires self-awareness, intentional choices, and a commitment to nurturing positive connections with yourself and others.

State of Emptiness

The concept of emptiness is found in various philosophical and spiritual traditions, each with its own interpretation and significance. Here are a few perspectives on the state of emptiness from different traditions:

1. **Buddhism:**

   – *Sunyata (Emptiness):* In Buddhism, particularly in the Mahayana tradition, the concept of Sunyata or emptiness is central. It refers to the idea that all phenomena lack inherent, independent existence. Emptiness is not nothingness but rather the absence of an intrinsic, unchanging essence. Understanding emptiness is a key aspect of attaining enlightenment.

2. **Taoism:**

   – *Wu Wei (Non-Action):* Taoist philosophy emphasises the concept of Wu Wei, often translated as "non-action" or "effortless action." It involves aligning oneself with the natural flow of the Tao (the Way) and allowing things to unfold spontaneously. This state of non-action is sometimes associated with a sense of emptiness, where the ego's control is relinquished.

3. **Zen Buddhism:**

   – *Mu (The Zen Koan):* In Zen Buddhism, the concept of emptiness is explored through the use of koans, such as "Mu," which means "nothing" or "emptiness." Meditating on Mu is meant to help the practitioner transcend conventional thinking and directly experience the state of emptiness beyond conceptual understanding.

4. **Christian Mysticism:**

   – *Apophatic Theology:* Some Christian mystics, particularly in the tradition of apophatic theology, explore the idea of encountering the divine through a form of "divine emptiness" or unknowing. This involves a direct experience of God that transcends intellectual understanding.

5. **Existentialism:**

   - *Jean-Paul Sartre:* Existentialist philosopher Jean-Paul Sartre used the term "emptiness" to describe the sense of existential void or nothingness that individuals may experience. In his view, individuals confront the emptiness of existence and must create their own meaning in a seemingly indifferent universe.

6. **Hermeticism:**

   - *Correspondence Principle:* In Hermeticism, the principle of correspondence suggests that there is a relationship between the macrocosm (the universe) and the microcosm (the individual). Emptiness, in this context, might refer to the idea that the individual is a reflection of the larger cosmic reality.

7. **Quantum Physics:**

   - *Quantum Vacuum:* In modern physics, the quantum vacuum is often described as a state of emptiness or the lowest energy state. This vacuum is not devoid of activity but is a dynamic field that gives rise to the fluctuations and manifestations of particles.

It's important to note that the concept of emptiness is nuanced and can have different meanings depending on the cultural, religious, or philosophical context. In many traditions, the experience of emptiness is not a negative state but rather a gateway to profound insight, liberation, or connection with a greater reality.

Karma

Karma is a concept rooted in Indian religions, primarily Hinduism, Buddhism, and Jainism. It refers to the law of cause and effect, where one's actions have consequences that affect one's present life and future existence. The understanding of karma varies among different traditions, but common elements include the idea that actions (karma) can influence the individual's destiny and shape their experiences in the cycle of life, death, and rebirth.

Here are key aspects of the concept of karma:

1. **Cause and Effect:**

   – Karma is based on the principle of cause and effect. Every action, whether physical, verbal, or mental, generates consequences.

Positive actions lead to positive results (good karma), while negative actions lead to negative results (bad karma).

2. **Reincarnation:**

   – The concept of karma is closely tied to the belief in reincarnation. Individuals are believed to undergo a cycle of rebirths, and the accumulated karma from previous lives influences the circumstances of their current and future lives.

3. **Moral Law:**

   – Karma is often seen as a moral law, governing not only actions but also intentions and motivations behind those actions. The quality of one's karma is influenced by the ethical and moral nature of their conduct.

4. **Dharma:**

   – Dharma refers to one's duty or righteous conduct. Following one's dharma is considered a way to accumulate positive karma. Each individual has a unique set of duties and responsibilities based on their role in society, and fulfilling these duties contributes to positive karma.

5. **Freedom and Responsibility:**

   – The concept of karma emphasises individual responsibility for one's actions. It suggests that individuals have the freedom to shape their destinies through their choices and behaviours.

6. **Purification and Liberation:**

   – Both Hinduism and Buddhism associate the accumulation of positive karma with spiritual progress. The ultimate goal is to purify the mind and soul from the cycle of rebirths (samsara) and attain liberation (moksha or Nirvana).

7. **Karmic Debts:**

   – Some traditions introduce the idea of karmic debts, suggesting that individuals may experience challenges or hardships in their current lives as a result of unresolved actions from past lives.

8. **Instant Karma:**

   – In some interpretations, karma is not solely bound to future lives but can also have more immediate effects. Actions may bring consequences in the present life, influencing the individual's well-being, relationships, and circumstances.

9. **Collective Karma:**

   – Karma is not limited to individual actions; it can also apply to groups, communities, and nations. Collective actions and their consequences contribute to the overall karmic fabric of a society.

It's important to note that while the concept of karma is deeply ingrained in Eastern philosophies, its interpretation and acceptance vary among individuals and communities. Some people view karma in a more literal and metaphysical sense, while others may see it as a metaphorical or psychological principle emphasising the ethical dimensions of human behaviour.

Spiritual Dimensions of Meditation

Meditation has deep spiritual dimensions that transcend its physical and mental benefits. Across various religious and philosophical traditions, meditation serves as a powerful tool for exploring and experiencing the spiritual aspects of human existence. Here are some key dimensions of meditation from a spiritual perspective:

1. **Inner Exploration and Self-Discovery:**
   - *Connection with the Self:* Meditation provides a space for individuals to connect with their inner selves, exploring the depths of consciousness.
   - *Unveiling Truths:* Through regular practice, meditators may uncover profound truths about themselves, their purpose, and their interconnectedness with the universe.
2. **Spiritual Awakening and Enlightenment:**
   - *Awakening the Soul:* Meditation is often regarded as a means to awaken the soul or higher self.
   - *Enlightenment:* In various spiritual traditions, deep meditation can lead to states of enlightenment, where individuals experience a profound shift in consciousness and perception.
3. **Connection with the Divine:**
   - *Communion with the Divine:* Many spiritual practices use meditation as a tool for communing with a higher power or divine presence.

– Divine Presence Within Some traditions emphasise finding the divine within oneself through introspection and meditation.

4. **Transcendence of Ego:**

   – *Ego Dissolution:* Meditation facilitates the transcending of the ego, allowing individuals to experience a state of oneness and unity with the cosmos.

   – *Identification with the Eternal:* By quieting the mind, meditation helps practitioners identify with the eternal aspect of their being rather than the transient ego.

5. **Mind-Body-Spirit Integration:**

   – *Holistic Well-Being:* Meditation is seen as a holistic practice that integrates the mind, body, and spirit.

   – *Alignment:* Spiritual traditions often emphasise the importance of aligning these aspects to achieve a balanced and harmonious existence.

6. **Enhanced Intuition and Insight:**

   – *Accessing Intuitive Wisdom:* Meditation is believed to open the gateway to intuitive insights and higher wisdom.

- *Clarity of Perception:* Practitioners often report heightened clarity of perception and a deep understanding of life's mysteries through regular meditation.

7. **Contemplation on Existence and Impermanence:**

   - *Contemplative Practices:* Meditation encourages contemplation on the nature of existence, impermanence, and the transient nature of life.

   - *Acceptance of Impermanence:* Spiritual meditation helps individuals come to terms with the impermanent nature of the material world.

8. **Emotional Healing and Compassion Cultivation:**

   - *Heart-Centred Practices:* Some meditation techniques focus on the heart centre, cultivating emotions like love and compassion.

   - *Healing:* Spiritual meditation can be a process of emotional healing, allowing individuals to release past traumas and negative emotions.

9. **Universal Connection and Unity Consciousness:**

   – *Interconnectedness:* Meditation fosters a sense of interconnectedness with all of creation.

   – *Unity Consciousness:* Spiritual meditators often seek to experience a state of unity consciousness, where the boundaries between self and the external world dissolve.

10. **Alignment with Higher Principles:**

   – *Moral and Ethical Development:* Meditation is considered a tool for aligning one's actions with higher moral and ethical principles.

   – Guidance from Within Spiritual meditation is seen as a means to receive guidance from within, leading individuals to make choices in alignment with their spiritual values.

11. **Mystical Experiences and Expanded Consciousness:**

   – *Opening to Mystical Realms:* Deep meditation can lead to mystical experiences where individuals feel a profound connection with the mystical dimensions of reality.

- *Expanded States of Consciousness:* Spiritual meditation may facilitate altered states of consciousness, opening the door to expanded awareness and perception.

12. Cultivation of Stillness and Silence:

- *Sacred Silence:* Many spiritual traditions consider the practice of silent meditation as a way to tap into the sacred and connect with the divine.

- *Stillness as a Gateway:* Stillness and silence are viewed as gateways to spiritual insights and higher states of consciousness.

13. Integration of Mindfulness into Daily Life:

- *Mindful Living:* Spiritual meditation encourages the integration of mindfulness into daily activities.

- *Presence in the Now:* Practitioners seek to carry the state of meditative awareness into their daily lives, fostering a continuous connection with the spiritual dimension.

14. Release of Attachments:

- *Detachment:* Meditation helps individuals release attachments to material possessions and transient desires.

- *Freedom from Clinging:* Spiritual meditation aims at cultivating a sense of inner freedom by letting go of attachments that bind the soul.

15. Service to Others and Compassionate Action:

- *Transcending Self-Interest:* Spiritual meditation often motivates individuals to engage in compassionate action and service to others.

- *Living Ethical Principles:* The insights gained through meditation guide practitioners to live ethically and contribute to the well-being of others.

16. Alignment with Cosmic Rhythms:

- *Tuning into Universal Forces:* Some spiritual traditions view meditation as a way to attune oneself to the natural rhythms and energies of the cosmos.

- *Harmonising with Existence:* Practitioners seek to harmonise their inner being with the larger cosmic order through meditative practices.

17. Connection with Ancestral Wisdom:

- *Ancestral Communication:* In certain spiritual practices, meditation is a means to connect with ancestral wisdom and receive guidance from the collective consciousness of ancestors.

- *Honouring Lineage:* Meditation is used to honour and acknowledge the spiritual lineage, drawing on the wisdom of those who came before.

18. Creation of Sacred Space:

- *Consecration of Space:* Meditation often involves creating a sacred space, whether internal or external.

- *Invoking the Sacred:* Practitioners may use rituals, symbols, or prayers to invoke the sacred within and around them during meditation.

19. **Integration with Rituals and Ceremonies:**

- *Ceremonial Practices:* Meditation is integrated into various ceremonial and ritualistic practices in spiritual traditions.
- *Sacramental Meditation:* Some traditions consider meditation a sacrament, a sacred act that connects individuals with divine energies.

20. **Moral Purification and Ethical Conduct:**

- *Purification of Mind and Heart:* Meditation serves as a tool for moral purification, cleansing the mind and heart of impurities.
- *Ethical Living:* Spiritual meditation guides individuals to live ethically and align their actions with higher moral principles.

In essence, the spiritual dimensions of meditation are diverse and multifaceted. The practice serves as a bridge between the material and spiritual realms, inviting individuals to explore the depths of their consciousness, connect with the divine, and cultivate a sense of unity with the cosmos. Whether approached through mindfulness, contemplation, or prayer, meditation offers a transformative journey that unfolds on the path to spiritual awakening and self-realisation

The Quest for Final Spiritual Enlightenment

Introduction

Spiritual enlightenment, often regarded as the pinnacle of human awakening, transcends the boundaries of religious dogma and cultural context. It represents the culmination of a profound inner journey, leading to the realisation of ultimate truth and the dissolution of the ego. Final spiritual enlightenment, in particular, denotes the attainment of a state of absolute awareness and unity with the divine. In this essay, we delve into the multifaceted dimensions of final spiritual enlightenment, exploring its nature, significance, pathways, challenges, and implications for individuals and society.

Understanding Final Spiritual Enlightenment

Final spiritual enlightenment is a state of consciousness characterised by profound clarity, inner peace, and unconditional love. It entails the recognition of the interconnectedness of all existence and the transcendence of dualistic thinking. At its core lies the dissolution of the ego, which is the primary obstacle to realising one's true nature as pure awareness.

In various spiritual traditions, the final spiritual enlightenment is described using different terminology. In Hinduism, it may be referred to as Moksha or Nirvana, representing liberation from the cycle of birth and death. In Buddhism, it is termed as Bodhi or Satori, signifying awakening to the true nature of reality. In mystical traditions such as Sufism and Kabbalah, it is depicted as a union with the divine or the realisation of God-consciousness.

Pathways to Final Spiritual Enlightenment

The journey towards final spiritual enlightenment encompasses a myriad of pathways, each tailored to the unique temperament and disposition of the seeker. While the ultimate destination remains the same, the routes vary based on cultural, religious, and personal factors. Some of the common pathways include:

1. **Meditation and Contemplative Practices:** Meditation serves as a foundational practice in many spiritual paths, enabling individuals to quiet the mind, cultivate mindfulness, and deepen their connection to the divine. Whether through focused attention, mindfulness, or

contemplation, meditation facilitates the direct experience of inner silence and transcendent states of consciousness.

2. **Self-Realisation and Self-Inquiry:** Engaging in self-inquiry involves questioning the nature of one's identity and seeking to uncover the true self beyond the egoic mind. Through practices such as introspection, journaling, and dialogue with spiritual teachers, individuals can penetrate the layers of conditioned beliefs and attachments, leading to profound insights into their true nature as pure awareness.

3. **Service and Compassion:** Acts of selfless service and compassion are integral to many spiritual paths, as they cultivate qualities such as empathy, kindness, and altruism. By serving others and alleviating the suffering of sentient beings, individuals can transcend their own egoic concerns and experience a deep sense of interconnectedness with all life.

4. **Devotion and Surrender:** Devotional practices, such as prayer, chanting, and ritual worship, are central to bhakti-oriented spiritual paths. Through heartfelt devotion and surrender to the divine, individuals can dissolve the illusion of

separateness and merge with the infinite love and wisdom of the cosmos.

Challenges on the Path to Final Spiritual Enlightenment

The journey towards final spiritual enlightenment is not without its challenges and obstacles. The ego, with its entrenched patterns of conditioning and resistance, poses a formidable barrier to realising one's true nature. Moreover, societal expectations, cultural norms, and external distractions can obscure the seeker's inner guidance and hinder their progress on the spiritual path.

Furthermore, the process of spiritual awakening often entails confronting deeply ingrained fears, traumas, and shadow aspects of the psyche. This inner work requires courage, honesty, and humility as individuals navigate the murky waters of their unconscious minds and integrate repressed emotions and memories.

Additionally, the pursuit of spiritual enlightenment may involve periods of doubt, confusion, and existential angst as individuals grapple with profound existential questions and the inherent uncertainty of the human condition. Moreover, the experience of spiritual awakening can be overwhelming and disorienting as individuals undergo radical shifts in consciousness and perception.

Implications of Final Spiritual Enlightenment

The realisation of final spiritual enlightenment has profound implications for the individual, as well as society as a whole. On a personal level, it brings about a radical transformation in consciousness, leading to inner peace, joy, and freedom from suffering. Moreover, it fosters a deep sense of connection to the divine and a profound reverence for all life.

At the societal level, final spiritual enlightenment has the potential to catalyse positive social change by fostering values such as compassion, empathy, and ecological stewardship. When individuals awaken to their true nature as interconnected beings, they are more inclined to act with integrity, kindness, and wisdom, thereby contributing to the collective welfare and the evolution of human consciousness.

Conclusion

The quest for final spiritual enlightenment is a profound and transformative journey, leading to the realisation of ultimate truth and the dissolution of the ego. While the paths leading to this ultimate realisation are diverse, they all share a common aim of transcending suffering and attaining inner peace. As individuals awaken to their true nature, they become catalysts for positive change, inspiring others to embark on the journey towards final spiritual enlightenment. Ultimately, the realisation of final spiritual enlightenment has the potential to transform not only the lives of individuals but also the fabric of society, ushering in an era of peace, harmony, and collective flourishing.

Illusion and Impermanance

Illusion and impermanence are foundational concepts in spirituality, providing profound insights into the nature of reality and the human condition. They are explored and elucidated across various spiritual traditions, offering guidance for seekers on their path towards spiritual awakening and enlightenment.

1. **Illusion (Maya, Samsara, or Mithya):**

   a. Maya in Hinduism:

   - Maya is a central concept in Hindu philosophy, particularly in Vedanta and Advaita Vedanta. It refers to the illusory nature of the world and the mistaken perception of separateness from the divine. Maya is considered the veiling power of Brahman, the ultimate reality.

   - According to Advaita Vedanta, Maya creates the multiplicity and diversity of the world, leading individuals to perceive themselves as separate entities distinct from the underlying unity of Brahman. This illusion of separation is the root cause of suffering.

- The goal of spiritual practice in Advaita Vedanta is to transcend Maya by realising one's essential identity with Brahman, thereby dispelling the illusion of duality and achieving liberation (moksha).

b. Samsara in Buddhism:

- In Buddhism, Samsara refers to the cycle of birth, death, and rebirth, characterised by suffering and impermanence. Samsara is perpetuated by ignorance (avijja) and craving (tanha), which bind individuals to the wheel of existence.

- The Buddha taught that the world is characterised by impermanence, suffering, and non-self (Anicca, Dukkha, Anatta). Samsara is considered the realm of illusion, where beings wander aimlessly, seeking happiness and fulfilment in transient phenomena.

- The path to liberation from Samsara involves developing insight into the three marks of existence (Anicca, Dukkha, Anatta) and cultivating wisdom (Prajna) to dispel the ignorance that perpetuates the cycle of rebirth.

c. Mithya in Advaita Vedanta:

- Mithya refers to the relative reality of the empirical world, which is neither entirely real (sat) nor entirely unreal (asat). According to Advaita Vedanta, the world is considered Mithya because it is subject to change and dependent on Brahman for its existence.

- Mithya does not imply complete negation of the world but rather a recognition of its conditional and transient nature. Individuals are encouraged to engage with the world while maintaining awareness of its illusory nature.

- The realisation of the ultimate reality (Brahman) leads to the understanding that the world, though appearing distinct and separate, is ultimately non-dual (Advaita).

This understanding liberates individuals from the bondage of illusion and grants them freedom (moksha).

2. **Impermanence (Anicca):**

a. Buddhist Perspective:

- Anicca, or impermanence, is one of the three marks of existence in Buddhism, alongside Dukkha (suffering) and Anatta (non-self). It is the recognition that all phenomena, whether material or mental, are transient and subject to change.

- The Buddha taught that attachment to impermanent phenomena leads to suffering. By clinging to things that are inherently fleeting, individuals experience disappointment, loss, and dissatisfaction.

- The contemplation of impermanence is a crucial aspect of Buddhist practice, as it cultivates wisdom (Prajna) and helps individuals develop detachment and equanimity. By embracing impermanence, practitioners can transcend suffering and achieve liberation (Nirvana).

b. Hindu Perspective:

- Impermanence is also acknowledged in Hinduism, albeit from a slightly different perspective. While Hinduism emphasises the eternal nature of the soul (Atman), it recognises the impermanence of the material world (Jagat).
- The concept of impermanence is intertwined with the cyclical nature of time (Kala) and the doctrine of Karma, which stipulates that all actions have consequences that unfold over time.
- In Hinduism, the realisation of impermanence serves as a catalyst for spiritual growth and detachment (Vairagya), leading individuals to seek liberation (moksha) from the cycle of birth and death (Samsara).

In conclusion, illusion (Maya, Samsara, or Mithya) and impermanence (Anicca) are profound concepts in spirituality that challenge individuals to question their perceptions of reality and the transient nature of existence. By recognising the illusory nature of the phenomenal world and embracing impermanence, seekers can transcend suffering and attain spiritual liberation. These concepts serve as guiding principles on the path towards enlightenment, offering profound insights into the nature of reality and the human condition.

Colours Seen in Deep Meditation Practices

In deep spiritual meditation practices, individuals may experience a wide range of visual phenomena, including colours. These experiences are subjective and can vary greatly from person to person. The perception of colours during meditation can be influenced by factors such as the individual's state of consciousness, level of concentration, and underlying psychological or physiological conditions. Here are some common experiences related to colours in deep spiritual meditation:

1. **Inner Light:**

   – Many practitioners report seeing an inner light or luminosity during deep meditation. This light is often described as bright, radiant, and suffused with a sense of peace and clarity. It may appear as white, golden, or translucent in colour, and is interpreted as a manifestation of spiritual energy or consciousness.

2. **Vivid Colours:**

   – Some meditators experience vivid and intense colours, which may appear as swirling patterns, geometric shapes, or pulsating hues. These colours can range from subtle pastels to vibrant primaries and are often perceived as dynamic and alive. The experience of vivid colours is associated with heightened states of awareness and concentration.

3. **Chakra Activation:**

   – In certain meditation practices, such as Kundalini or chakra meditation, practitioners focus on activating and harmonising the body's energy centres known as chakras. Each chakra is associated with a specific colour, and during meditation, individuals may visualise or perceive these colours corresponding to the respective chakras. For example, red is for the root chakra, and orange is for the sacral chakra, yellow is for the solar plexus chakra, and so on.

4. **Symbolic Imagery:**

   – Colours may also appear in meditation as symbolic imagery or archetypal symbols representing aspects of the practitioner's inner landscape or spiritual journey. For instance, blue might symbolise tranquillity and wisdom, while green could represent growth and healing. These symbolic associations can vary depending on the individual's cultural background, personal beliefs, and spiritual tradition.

5. **Transcendent Light:**

   – In advanced stages of meditation or mystical experiences, individuals may encounter experiences of transcendent light, which surpass ordinary perception and comprehension. This light is often described as ineffable, infinite, and imbued with divine presence. It transcends conventional notions of colour and form, representing the ultimate reality or source of existence.

It's important to note that the perception of colours during meditation is not the primary goal of spiritual practice but rather a byproduct of deepening concentration, mindfulness, and inner exploration. While these experiences can be profound and transformative, practitioners are encouraged to maintain a balanced and non-attached attitude towards them, recognising them as transient manifestations of the mind's activity on the path towards greater spiritual realisation.

Connection With the Soul of the Guru Through Meditation

Meditation can indeed serve as a powerful means of establishing a connection with the soul of a guru or spiritual teacher. This connection is often experienced as a deepening of one's spiritual guidance, inspiration, and understanding. Here's how meditation can facilitate this connection:

1. **Intention Setting:** Before beginning the meditation, practitioners often set the intention to connect with the wisdom, presence, and guidance of their guru or spiritual teacher. This intention acts as a focal point for the meditation practice, directing the individual's attention towards the desired connection.

2. **Visualisation:** Many meditation practices involve visualising the presence of the guru or spiritual teacher in front of them. This visualisation can take various forms, such as

imagining the guru's radiant light or envisioning their physical form sitting or standing before the practitioner. The visualisation serves to strengthen the sense of connection and receptivity to the guru's energy and teachings.

3. **Mantra or Affirmations:** Some practitioners use mantras or affirmations related to their guru or spiritual teacher during meditation. By chanting the guru's name, a sacred mantra, or affirming their teachings, practitioners can invoke their presence and guidance more deeply into their consciousness. This repetition helps to focus the mind and attune it to the guru's vibration.

4. **Silent Communication:** In meditation, practitioners may engage in silent communication with their guru or spiritual teacher, expressing gratitude, seeking guidance, or simply being present with their presence. This silent dialogue can foster a profound sense of connection and intimacy, transcending verbal communication and accessing deeper levels of insight and understanding.

5. **Heart-Centred Awareness:** Meditation practices often emphasise cultivating heart-

centred awareness, wherein practitioners open their hearts to receive and transmit love, compassion, and wisdom. By directing their awareness towards the heart centre and invoking the presence of the guru, practitioners can establish a direct connection with the guru's soul, which is said to reside in the heart of every being.

6. **Inner Journey:** Through meditation, practitioners can embark on an inner journey to explore the depths of their own consciousness and connect with the universal source of wisdom and guidance. In this state of expanded awareness, the boundaries between self and other, teacher and student, dissolve, revealing the underlying unity of existence.

7. **Integration and Application:** The connection established through meditation with the soul of the guru is not confined to the meditation cushion but extends into daily life. Practitioners can integrate the insights and guidance received during meditation into their thoughts, words, and actions, thereby embodying the teachings of their guru in their everyday existence.

In summary, meditation serves as a powerful tool for establishing a connection with the soul of a guru or spiritual teacher, enabling practitioners to receive guidance, inspiration, and support on their spiritual journey. Through intention, visualisation, mantra, silent communication, heart-centred awareness, inner journey, and integration, practitioners can deepen their relationship with their guru and access the profound wisdom and compassion that lie at the core of their teachings.

Death and Cyclic Rebirth

Death holds significant importance in spirituality across various traditions, often viewed as a transition rather than an endpoint. Here's a detailed explanation of death in spirituality:

1. **Impermanence and Transience:**

   – In many spiritual traditions, including Buddhism and Hinduism, impermanence (Anicca) is recognised as a fundamental aspect of existence. Death is seen as a natural consequence of impermanence, highlighting the transient nature of all phenomena. Rather than fearing death, spiritual teachings emphasise embracing impermanence as a reminder to live fully and mindfully in the present-moment.

2. **Cycle of Rebirth:**

   – In traditions such as Hinduism, Buddhism, and Jainism, death is viewed as a part of the cycle of rebirth (Samsara). According to these beliefs, the soul (Atman or Jiva) undergoes a series of births and deaths propelled by the force of karma. Each life presents an opportunity for spiritual growth and liberation (Moksha or Nirvana), with death marking the transition between one incarnation and the next.

3. **Ego Dissolution:**

   - Spiritual teachings often emphasise the importance of transcending the ego or the false sense of self. Death is seen as the ultimate dissolution of the ego, as the physical body and personal identity are shed. Through practices such as meditation and self-inquiry, individuals can prepare for death by cultivating a deeper understanding of the impermanence of the ego and the underlying continuity of consciousness.

4. **The Great Mystery:**

   - Death is regarded as one of life's greatest mysteries, transcending the limitations of human understanding. Spiritual traditions often approach death with humility and reverence, acknowledging the ineffable nature of the transition from life to death.

Rather than seeking definitive answers, practitioners are encouraged to embrace the mystery of death as an invitation to explore the deeper dimensions of existence.

5. **Preparation and Transition:**

   – Many spiritual traditions offer guidance and practices to support individuals in preparing for death and navigating the transition with grace and awareness. Practices such as death meditation, contemplation of impermanence, and recollection of virtuous actions (merit) are common ways to cultivate acceptance and peace in the face of death. Additionally, rituals and ceremonies surrounding death provide opportunities for community support and spiritual reflection.

6. **Continuity of Consciousness:**

   – While the physical body may perish, spiritual teachings often affirm the continuity of consciousness beyond death. The soul or essence of the individual is believed to transcend the limitations of the body, embarking on a journey of spiritual evolution and exploration. This perspective offers solace and comfort to those grappling with the loss of loved ones, knowing that the bond of love transcends the boundaries of life and death.

7. **Transformation and Liberation:**

   - Ultimately, death is viewed as a gateway to transformation and liberation in many spiritual traditions. It is seen as an opportunity for the soul to transcend the cycle of suffering and attain union with the divine or ultimate reality. By embracing death as a natural and inevitable part of the human experience, individuals can cultivate greater peace, wisdom, and liberation in both life and death.

In summary, death holds profound significance in spirituality, serving as a reminder of impermanence, a catalyst for spiritual growth, and a gateway to transformation and liberation. By embracing death with awareness, humility, and reverence, individuals can navigate the transition with grace and cultivate deeper insights into the nature of existence and consciousness.

The Divine Light Through the Eye

The concept of experiencing divine light through the eyes is a profound and mystical phenomenon described in various spiritual traditions and mystical experiences. Here's a detailed exploration of this concept:

1. **Symbolism and Metaphor:**

   – In many spiritual traditions, light is used as a symbol of divine presence, wisdom, and enlightenment. The eyes, as the windows to the soul, are believed to be conduits for perceiving and embodying this divine light. Metaphorically, experiencing divine light through the eyes represents a direct encounter with the divine, an awakening of inner vision, and a recognition of one's innate divinity.

2. **Mystical Experiences:**

   – Mystics and spiritual seekers throughout history have reported profound experiences of divine light manifesting through their eyes during moments of deep meditation, prayer, or ecstatic states. This divine light is often described as radiant, luminous, and imbued with a sense of bliss, love, and transcendence. It is perceived not only as an external phenomenon but also as an inner illumination that illuminates the depths of consciousness.

3. **Inner Light and Enlightenment:**

   – In spiritual traditions such as Hinduism, Buddhism, and Sufism, the experience of inner light (Jyoti, Prakash, Noor) is considered a sign of spiritual awakening and enlightenment. Through practices such as meditation, contemplation, and devotion, practitioners may cultivate the ability to perceive this inner light directly within themselves, illuminating the path towards self-realisation and union with the divine.

4. **Divine Gaze and Blessings:**

   – In some mystical traditions, saints, sages, and spiritual masters are believed to possess the power to transmit divine light through their gaze, known as the "divine gaze" or "spiritual transmission." Those who receive this gaze may experience profound transformation, healing, and awakening as the divine light penetrates their being, dispelling darkness and igniting the flame of spiritual realisation.

5. **Universal Consciousness:**

   – The experience of divine light through the eyes is often interpreted as a glimpse into the interconnectedness of all existence and the unity of consciousness. In this state of expanded awareness, individuals may perceive themselves as vessels for the divine light, participating in the unfolding of cosmic evolution and the realisation of universal love and harmony.

6. **Integration and Embodiment:**

   – While experiencing divine light through the eyes can be a profound and transcendent experience, spiritual teachings emphasise the importance of integrating and embodying this light in everyday life. Rather than seeking external manifestations of enlightenment, practitioners are encouraged to cultivate inner clarity, compassion, and wisdom, allowing the divine light to illuminate their thoughts, words, and actions.

7. **Unity of Opposites:**

   – The experience of divine light through the eyes reflects the unity of opposites, transcending dualities such as light and darkness, form and formlessness, self and other. It signifies the reconciliation of individual consciousness with universal consciousness, leading to a profound sense of oneness, peace, and wholeness.

In summary, experiencing divine light through the eyes is a mystical phenomenon that symbolises spiritual awakening, enlightenment, and union with the divine. Whether encountered through inner illumination, mystical experiences, or the gaze of a spiritual master, this divine light serves as a beacon of truth, love, and transcendence, guiding seekers on their journey towards self-realisation and ultimate liberation.

The Compassion and Communication With Soul

Compassion and communication with the soul are deeply interconnected aspects of spiritual practice and inner growth. Here's a detailed exploration of how compassion fosters communication with the soul:

1. **Compassion as a Bridge:**

   - Compassion serves as a bridge between the individual's egoic self and their soul or higher self. By cultivating compassion towards oneself and others, individuals create an environment of acceptance, love, and understanding within which communication with the soul can occur. Compassion softens the barriers of ego and opens the heart to the wisdom and guidance of the soul.

2. **Deep Listening:**

   - Compassionate communication with the soul begins with deep listening. This involves quieting the mind, opening the heart, and attuning to the subtle whispers of intuition, inspiration, and inner guidance. Through the practice of mindfulness and presence, individuals create space for the soul's messages to be heard and integrated into their awareness.

3. **Self-Compassion:**

   – Self-compassion is an essential aspect of communicating with the soul. It involves treating oneself with kindness, gentleness, and understanding, especially during times of struggle, doubt, or uncertainty. By nurturing a compassionate attitude towards oneself, individuals create a supportive inner environment conducive to soul communication and self-discovery.

4. **Empathy and Connection:**

   – Compassion fosters empathy and connection with others, which in turn enhances communication with the soul. As individuals cultivate empathy towards the experiences and emotions of others, they develop a deeper understanding of universal human suffering and interconnectedness. This empathic resonance opens the heart to the collective wisdom and compassion of the soul.

5. **Alignment with Higher Values:**

   – Compassionate communication with the soul aligns individuals with their higher values and spiritual aspirations. By embodying qualities such as kindness, generosity, and forgiveness, individuals attune themselves to the vibrational frequency of the soul, allowing its wisdom and guidance to flow more freely into their consciousness.

6. **Healing and Transformation:**

   – Compassion acts as a catalyst for healing and transformation at the soul level. By approaching oneself and others with compassion, individuals create opportunities for healing past wounds, releasing limiting beliefs and embracing greater levels of self-awareness and authenticity. This process of inner healing opens the channels of communication with the soul, facilitating a deeper integration of its wisdom and love.

7. **Service and Altruism:**

   - Compassionate action and service to others are powerful ways to deepen communication with the soul. Engaging in acts of kindness, generosity, and altruism allows individuals to embody the soul's inherent qualities of love and compassion in the world. Through selfless service, individuals dissolve the barriers of ego and align themselves with the greater purpose and meaning of their soul's journey.

8. **Gratitude and Reverence:**

   - Compassionate communication with the soul is nurtured through gratitude and reverence for the mysteries of existence. By cultivating a sense of awe and appreciation for the beauty and interconnectedness of all life, individuals attune themselves to the sacredness of their soul's journey and the guidance it offers along the way.

In summary, compassion is both a pathway to and an expression of communication with the soul. By cultivating compassion towards oneself, others, and all of creation, individuals create the conditions for deep listening, empathy, alignment with higher values, healing, and transformation. Through compassionate action and service, individuals embody the wisdom and love of their souls, enriching their lives and the lives of others with their boundless grace and beauty.

Changes in Behaviour and Lifestyle Through Meditation

Meditation can bring about profound changes in behaviour and lifestyle, leading to greater well-being, clarity, and fulfilment. Here's a detailed exploration of the transformative effects of meditation:

1. **Stress Reduction:**

   – Meditation is well-known for its ability to reduce stress levels by activating the relaxation response in the body. Through regular practice, individuals learn to cultivate a sense of calm and equanimity, even in the face of life's challenges. This reduction in stress can lead to improvements in mood, sleep, and overall mental health.

2. **Emotional Regulation:**

   – Meditation helps individuals develop greater emotional awareness and regulation. By observing their thoughts and emotions with mindfulness, practitioners learn to respond to stimuli rather than react impulsively. This enhanced emotional resilience allows individuals to navigate difficult emotions with greater ease and compassion towards themselves and others.

3. **Increased Focus and Concentration:**

   – Meditation strengthens the capacity for sustained attention and concentration. Through practices such as focused attention or mindfulness meditation, individuals train their minds to remain present and attentive to the task at hand. This sharpened focus can enhance productivity, creativity, and overall cognitive performance.

4. **Enhanced Self-awareness:**

   – Meditation cultivates greater self-awareness by encouraging individuals to observe their thoughts, emotions, and bodily sensations without judgement. This heightened self-awareness allows individuals to recognise habitual patterns of behaviour and thought, empowering them to make conscious choices aligned with their values and aspirations.

5. **Improved Relationships:**

   – Meditation fosters deeper connections and empathy in relationships. By cultivating qualities such as compassion, patience, and non-reactivity, individuals become more attuned to the needs and experiences of others. This enhanced interpersonal sensitivity leads to more harmonious and fulfilling relationships with family, friends, and colleagues.

6. **Mindful Eating and Lifestyle Choices:**

   – Meditation encourages mindful eating and lifestyle choices, promoting greater awareness of the body's signals of hunger, satiety, and nutritional needs. By practicing mindful eating, individuals develop a healthier relationship with food, savouring each bite and making choices that nourish their body and spirit. Similarly, mindfulness extends to other areas of life, such as exercise, sleep, and leisure activities, fostering a balanced and holistic approach to well-being.

7. **Strengthened Resilience and Coping Skills:**

   – Meditation builds resilience and coping skills in the face of adversity. By cultivating a sense of inner stability and resourcefulness, individuals develop the capacity to bounce back from setbacks and challenges with greater ease and grace. This resilience enables individuals to navigate life's ups and downs with equanimity and courage.

8. **Spiritual Growth and Transformation:**

   – Meditation can catalyse profound spiritual growth and transformation. As individuals deepen their practice, they may experience insights, intuitions, and states of consciousness that transcend the ordinary mind. This spiritual awakening fosters a deeper sense of connection with oneself, others, and the universe, leading to greater wisdom, compassion, and inner peace.

In summary, meditation can lead to a wide range of positive changes in behaviour and lifestyle, including stress reduction, emotional regulation, increased focus, enhanced self-awareness, improved relationships, mindful eating and lifestyle choices, strengthened resilience, and spiritual growth. By incorporating meditation into their daily routine, individuals can cultivate greater well-being, clarity, and fulfilment in all areas of life.

The Reality Between Life and Death

The reality between life and death is a profound and enigmatic aspect of existence that has fascinated philosophers, mystics, and scientists for millennia. Here's a detailed exploration of this complex topic:

1. **Interconnectedness of Life and Death:**

    – Life and death are two inseparable aspects of the same continuum. While life is characterised by growth, change, and vitality, death represents the cessation of biological functions and the transition to a different state of existence. In many spiritual traditions, life and death are seen as interconnected and cyclical, with each influencing and giving rise to the other.

2. **Impermanence and Change:**

   – Central to the reality between life and death is the recognition of impermanence (Anicca). All phenomena, including life itself, are subject to constant change and flux. Birth and death are natural manifestations of this universal law of impermanence, reminding us of the transient nature of existence and the inevitability of change.

3. **Mystery and Uncertainty:**

   – Despite advances in science and philosophy, the reality between life and death remains shrouded in mystery and uncertainty. The nature of consciousness, the afterlife, and the ultimate fate of the individual beyond death are questions that continue to elude definitive answers. This inherent mystery invites contemplation, wonder, and humility in the face of the unknown.

4. **Cultural and Religious Perspectives:**

   – Cultural and religious perspectives shape how individuals understand and interpret the reality between life and death. In some traditions, such as Buddhism and

Hinduism, death is viewed as a transition to another realm of existence governed by the law of karma and rebirth. In others, such as Christianity and Islam, death is seen as a passage to an afterlife, where individuals are judged according to their beliefs and actions in life.

5. **Existential Reflection:**

   – The reality between life and death prompts existential reflection on the meaning and purpose of existence. Confronting the reality of mortality encourages individuals to contemplate their values, priorities, and legacy. This reflection can inspire a deeper appreciation for the preciousness of life and a commitment to living authentically and meaningfully.

6. **Integration of Life and Death:**

   – Spiritual wisdom teaches the importance of integrating the reality of death into the fabric of life. By acknowledging the impermanence of existence and the inevitability of death, individuals can live more fully and authentically, cherishing each moment and embracing the richness of human experience. This integration fosters a sense of acceptance, gratitude, and equanimity in the face of life's uncertainties.

7. **Transformation and Renewal:**

   – The reality between life and death is also associated with themes of transformation and renewal. Just as death marks the end of one phase of existence, it also heralds the beginning of another. In the cycle of birth, death, and rebirth, there is the potential for growth, evolution, and spiritual awakening. Death, therefore, is not only an ending but also a gateway to new possibilities and dimensions of being.

8. **Embracing the Mystery:**

   – Ultimately, the reality between life and death invites individuals to embrace the mystery of existence with humility, curiosity, and awe. Rather than seeking definitive answers or explanations, there is value in dwelling in the mystery itself, allowing it to inspire wonder, creativity, and a deeper appreciation for the ineffable beauty of life and consciousness.

In summary, the reality between life and death is a multifaceted and profound aspect of existence that invites contemplation, reflection, and awe. It encompasses themes of impermanence, interconnectedness, mystery, transformation, and renewal, reminding us of the preciousness and mystery of life itself. By embracing the reality between life and death with openness and curiosity, individuals can cultivate greater wisdom, compassion, and appreciation for the profound mystery of existence.

Rebirth

1. **Cycle of Samsara:**

   - Rebirth is a central tenet of the cycle of Samsara, the continuous cycle of birth, death, and rebirth in Hinduism, Buddhism, and Jainism. According to this belief, beings are bound to the cycle of Samsara by the force of karma, the law of cause and effect, which determines the circumstances of each successive incarnation.

2. **Karma and Rebirth:**

   - Karma plays a crucial role in the process of rebirth. It is believed that individuals accumulate karma, both positive and negative, through their thoughts, words, and actions in each lifetime. This accumulated karma influences the conditions of their next incarnation, determining factors such as social status, physical health, and life circumstances.

3. **Purpose of Rebirth:**

   – The purpose of rebirth varies among different spiritual traditions. In Hinduism, rebirth offers opportunities for spiritual growth, learning, and the fulfilment of karmic debts. In Buddhism, rebirth is seen as an opportunity to progress on the path to enlightenment (Nirvana) by cultivating virtues such as wisdom, compassion, and ethical conduct. In Jainism, rebirth is viewed as a means to purify the soul (Jiva) and attain liberation (Moksha) from the cycle of Samsara.

4. **Transmigration of Souls:**

   – Rebirth encompasses the transmigration of souls from one body to another. The soul, known as Atman in Hinduism and Jainism, or consciousness in Buddhism, is believed to be eternal and indestructible, undergoing a continuous process of birth and rebirth across different lifetimes and realms of existence.

5. **Rebirth in Different Realms:**

   – According to some spiritual traditions, rebirth can occur in different realms or planes of existence, including heavenly realms, human realms, animal realms, and hellish realms. The conditions of each realm are determined by the individual's karma and spiritual evolution, with higher realms offering greater opportunities for spiritual advancement.

6. **Rebirth and Liberation:**

   – The ultimate goal of rebirth is liberation from the cycle of Samsara and the attainment of spiritual realisation or enlightenment. In Hinduism, liberation (Moksha) is achieved through the realisation of one's true nature, which is identical to Brahman's ultimate reality. In Buddhism, liberation (Nirvana) is attained by extinguishing the causes of suffering and ignorance, thereby ending the cycle of rebirth.

7. **Evidence and Controversy:**

   – The concept of rebirth is a subject of debate and controversy, particularly in the context of empirical evidence and scientific inquiry. While anecdotal accounts, near-death experiences, and past-life memories have been cited as suggestive of rebirth, conclusive scientific proof remains elusive. Sceptics argue that such phenomena can be explained by psychological factors, cultural influences, and the fallibility of memory.

8. **Personal Beliefs and Interpretations:**

   – Beliefs about rebirth vary widely among individuals and cultures, influenced by religious upbringing, cultural traditions, and personal experiences. For many people, the belief in rebirth provides a framework for understanding the complexities of existence, offering hope, meaning, and a sense of continuity beyond the confines of a single lifetime.

In summary, rebirth is a profound and complex concept found in various religious and spiritual traditions, reflecting humanity's enduring quest for understanding the nature of existence and the mysteries of life and death. Whether viewed as a literal truth, a metaphorical symbol, or a philosophical hypothesis, rebirth continues to inspire contemplation, inquiry, and debate about the nature of consciousness, karma, and the ultimate purpose of human existence.

www.ingramcontent.com/pod-product-compliance
Lightning Source LLC
LaVergne TN
LVHW091253150826
845673LV00006B/1396

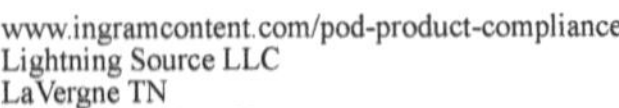

* 9 7 9 8 8 9 3 6 3 3 4 0 5 *